MW00397409

Righteous
A 40-day journey through Romans

Bob Perdue
LifeNow Ministries
www.lifenowministries.com

September 2014

Acknowledgements

Honor to whom honor is due

I would like to thank Eddie Gallion for his faith in me as a spiritual leader, teacher of truth and writer. He funded this project and challenged me to write during a very difficult time in my life and the project proved instrumental to my own healing.

I would also like to thank Esther Booth for the hours of editing she put in to correct my grammar and eliminate my many exclamation points!!!!!!

I gleaned a lot of information for this book by listening to sermon series on Romans from both Ray Stedman and Dr. Andrew Farley, so I want to think them for their diligent study.

Another big thank you goes to my Sunday night Bible Study group who have walked with me through some of this study and helped me re-work different sections to be more helpful for the reader. Thank you Doug, Cheryl, Mark, Cheryl, Jeff, Neva, Doug, Lillian and Terri.

Preface

Romans has often been called the most theological of all of Paul's epistles. For this reason, many Christians prefer to study shorter, more easily understood epistles like Philippians or Ephesians. This is a tragedy because Romans is truly a book filled with rich and encouraging truth to the believer. Paul actually writes this book, not to burden us with heavy doctrine, but to assure us that the Gospel is truly the answer to all of our problems!

Romans was written as a narrative to first century believers who were struggling with the differences between the Old Covenant (the law) and the New Covenant (grace). Every verse in this book must be seen as a part of that larger narrative. Extracting verses out of context to support a certain theological grid violates the text and distorts the message.

In Romans 1-11 Paul will establish the New Covenant or Gospel message that righteousness is by grace (a free gift from God) given to us when we put our faith in the finished work of Christ on the cross. In Romans 12-16, Paul will give us a picture of what living out righteousness looks like in this world.

The study is designed to be completed in 40 days. Each chapter begins with a passage from Romans and contains instructions for marking up the text in order to make initial connections that come right out of the Scripture. After each section is marked, the reading helps to pull it all together. At the end of each chapter are a few questions that can be used in a small group setting.

All Bible references in this book are taken from the New International Version.
Holy Bible, New International Version®, NIV® Copyright ©
1973, 1978, 1984, 2011 by Biblica, Inc.®

Day 1

◆◆◆◆◆◆◆◆◆◆◆◆◆◆◆◆◆◆◆◆◆◆

Introduction

Recently, I decided to hike along a nature trail in the mountains of western North Carolina to spend some quiet time with God. The trail looked long, difficult, and strenuous, and I knew this wasn't going to be an easy hike. At the entrance to the trail, there was information about what I might encounter along the way; wetlands, a dry riverbed, different species of trees, flowers and plants, as well as possible sightings of wildlife. The information interested me; it whet my appetite and motivated me to continue on the trail. It also provided an informed vigilance that trained my eye to look for certain things along the way.

We are going to take a walk together through the book of Romans. Romans is a deep book filled with theology and a lot of big words. You may be thinking just what I was thinking at the beginning of that trail. This is not going to be an easy stroll. Let me give you a little information about what you will encounter along this path. I believe this will interest you, whet your appetite, and motivate you to join me on my walk through Romans.

There are several words found in the book of Romans that appear more often than in any other book of the Bible. These words become clues to the message of Romans. In fact, we can connect all of these words together to summarize the message that Paul was communicating when he wrote this letter to the church at Rome around 60 AD.

One of the words we will encounter frequently in this book is the word **righteousness.** The Greek word *dikaiosuna* literally means "one who is as he ought to be, one who is right, not simply in what he does but in who he is." In reference to our relationship with God, righteousness is the condition of being accepted by God, completely. It is experiencing the life God always intended for us.

I believe we all have a desire for life built into us by God and a drive to experience that life. Living in a righteous relationship with God is life. Another form of the same Greek word is translated "justification" throughout Romans. This word means to make someone righteous or to declare or deem them righteous. I don't know about you, but this interests me, actually excites me. I have often had thoughts like "something isn't quite right or there has to be more to life than this." I have often felt rejected and unaccepted because of some weakness or flaw in my character. Hearing that there is a way to be as I ought to be or to be who I was created to be is exciting. So as we stroll through this book, be on the lookout for righteousness.

Another word used more often in Romans is **grace**. The Greek word *charis* means "favor or merciful kindness". It is goodwill that flows out of the character of the One who gives that is not motivated by anything in the one who receives. Scripture says that "God is love" (I John 4:8). It is His nature to love. Grace flows out of His love and makes it possible for God to initiate relationship with sinful man. There is nothing good in man that prompts God's grace; it flows 100% out of God's love (and Paul will go to great lengths to make this point throughout Romans). Grace is God's operating system and is the evidence of His love for us. Because of our sin, God can only relate to us through His grace. Often we struggle with the feeling that God is upset with us because of our behavior. This feeling hinders our ability to approach Him or practice His presence in our daily life. Encountering grace is like a breath of fresh air because it releases us from striving and performing. We will be able to breathe it in more than 20 times through this book.

The next word used often in Romans is the word **faith**. The Greek word *pistis* means the "conviction of the truth of something." The words "believe" or "belief" are often used to translate this word as well. When you hear about the wonderful concepts of grace and righteousness, your humanity immediately wants to know what you can do to experience these things. The truth is that you can't DO anything; you must simply believe, or have faith. There is no striving, trying to do better, or working hard for God's grace and righteousness. Life as it was always meant to be is a gift from Him and is simply received as we believe (faith). All of a sudden this hike through Romans is starting to feel a little easier because it is by grace through faith!

The final word I want us to be on the lookout for as we stroll through Paul's letter to the Romans is the word **Gospel**. The Greek word is *euangellion*. This is a compound word. The prefix eu means "good" or "well." The word angellion means "message" and is related to the word for angel which means "messenger." The Gospel is the good message of Christ's death, burial, and resurrection to pay the price for our sins. It is the central focus of Paul's message. So as we walk along through this book, expect to hear some really good news, something that will encourage us!

How do these four words relate to each other? What message is Paul communicating to us through the repeated use of these words? If we put these words all together in a single thought, it might look like this:

The Gospel or good news of Christ's death, burial and resurrection for us is given to us by God's grace. We receive the Gospel by faith or by believing it and the result is that we are made righteous or justified, becoming fully connected to and accepted by God and able to experience the life God always intended.

Or

I become completely acceptable to God (righteous) by believing (faith) in the sacrifice of Christ for my sin (Gospel) and it is absolutely free (grace).

Enjoy your walk!

Day 2

••••••••••••••••••••••••••

Travelling Companions
(Romans 1:1-7)

1 Paul, a servant of Christ Jesus, called to be an apostle and set apart for the gospel of God— 2 the gospel he promised beforehand through his prophets in the Holy Scriptures 3 regarding his Son, who as to his human nature was a descendant of David, 4 and who through the Spirit of holiness was declared with power to be the Son of God by his resurrection from the dead: Jesus Christ our Lord. 5 Through him we received grace and apostleship to call all the Gentiles to the obedience that comes from faith for his name's sake. 6 And you also are among those who are called to belong to Jesus Christ. 7 To all in Rome who are loved by God and called to be saints: Grace and peace to you from God our Father and from the Lord Jesus Christ.

If we are going on a walk or a hike, we would want to know where we are going and what we might see along the way. However, what may be even more important is to know who is walking with us. I know there are some people that I wouldn't want to take along with me, especially if I wanted some quiet!

In the introduction to Romans, we meet three people that will be travelling with us on this stroll. In verse 1, we are introduced to Paul, the author of the book. In verse 3, we are introduced to Jesus who will obviously play a significant role in the discussion along the way. Finally in verse 6, we meet the Roman Christians to whom this book is written. Let's get to know our travelling companions by examining their introduction in these verses.

> *Circle the world* **Paul** *(1). Now circle the words* **servant, called, apostle** *and* **set apart** *(1). Draw a box around the word* **Gospel** *(1).*

The Apostle Paul

Paul defines himself first and foremost as a servant of Christ Jesus (v1). The word servant literally means a bond slave or one who gives himself up for the benefit and interest of another. The word denotes more the position than it does the duty. In other words, being a bond slave of Jesus is not primarily about what we do for Him but who we are in relationship to Him. In the account of Paul's conversion in Acts 9, he became a bond slave of Jesus when God said, *Now get up and go into the city and you will be told what you must do* (Acts 9:6). Paul immediately assumed the position of a bond slave, submitted himself to Christ as Master and did exactly as God commanded. Out of the posture of a bond slave flows devoted service that is neither drudgery nor duty.

In relationship to Jesus, Paul is a bond slave, but in relationship to the Christians at Rome he is an *apostle* (v1). The word is first used in the New Testament in Luke 6:13 when Jesus chose his 12 disciples. *When morning came, he called his disciples to him and chose twelve of them, whom he also designated apostles.* An apostle is a messenger, one who is sent like a delegate to represent and deliver the message of another. The apostles of the New Testament were a distinct group that personally saw the resurrected Christ and were commissioned by Him to be witnesses. This is clearly true of the original 12 (John 15:27; Acts 1:8, 21), but in a unique way was true of Paul as well. In relating his conversion experience to King Agrippa in Acts 26, Paul records that Jesus said to him, *I have appeared to you to appoint you as a servant and as a witness of what you have seen of me and what I will show you* (v16). Paul was introducing himself to the Roman Christians whom he had never met first as servant but then as an apostle in order to establish his authority to say the things that he needed to say to them. This introduction of himself is fairly consistent through all of his epistles, establishing his authority in order to give credence to his message. It is like a police officer showing his badge to establish his authority over a certain situation.

Finally, Paul uses the words *called* and *set apart* to describe himself. He was called to be an apostle. He did not seek apostleship, work toward apostleship, strive to be an apostle, or go to apostle school. He was invited by God to be an apostle. Saul (as he was known before his conversion) was a Pharisee, a Jewish leader, and passionately opposed the Christ followers. In Acts 9, he was on his way to Damascus to persecute Christians when he was personally confronted with the resurrected Christ and invited to be His witness to the Gentiles. Paul was already a highly regarded student of the law, a leader in the Jewish community, and known for his study and spotless reputation. Those are the things that Paul spent his time working hard to achieve in his life before his encounter with Christ. The position and authority he held in the Jewish community was something he earned by his own study, effort, and striving. In contrast, his position and authority as a Christian was not earned. Paul was invited into it, not based on his previous strivings but, some might say, in spite of them. He was not commanded to do the works of an apostle (religion), he was invited to be a follower of Jesus and share His message (relationship). The works of an apostle would not require striving but would flow out of this relationship. Paul initiated the process that led him to be a leader in the Jewish community, but God initiated this calling. This is grace. Remember that grace is the favor or merciful kindness of God that flows out of His love. In fact, a few verses later Paul puts grace and apostleship together when he says, *we received grace and apostleship to call people from among the Gentiles...*(1:5). Neither grace nor apostleship is something that can be earned; they are simply received.

Paul was *called* to be an apostle or a messenger for God in a general sense, but he was *set apart* or marked off specifically to be a messenger of the Gospel. Here is one of those words we were alerted to at the beginning of our trail. The Gospel or the good news of the death, burial, and resurrection of Christ was the specific message that Paul, as an apostle, was appointed to share.

Throughout Romans it becomes clear that the Roman Christians had a tendency to get off track and prioritize something other than the Gospel. The Jewish believers in the church were very proud of their heritage. They had been the chief recipients of the Old Covenant or Mosaic Law. This system of rules and regulations given by God at Mount Sinai was Judaism. However, the Gospel was a New Covenant. No longer would man try to meet God's righteous standard by obedience to the law (Old Covenant), but they would simply put their faith in Christ's death, burial, and resurrection (Gospel or New Covenant). Obedience and striving was engrained in these people, but Paul continually brought them back to the Gospel. We also live in a culture where striving, performance, and self-promotion are valued and rewarded. Whether in school, in sports, on the job or even in church, we are taught to strive to be the best. The Gospel is counter-cultural, which makes it hard for us to receive. One of the problems of the modern church is that our culture continually creeps into the Gospel message bringing striving, judgment, hypocrisy, and division.

Paul strengthened the Gospel message for them by reminding them that the Gospel was ...*promised beforehand through his prophets in the Holy Scriptures....* (v2). There are over 50 references to the Old Testament in the book of Romans. The Gospel is not some new message that moves in quickly to replace the old. The Gospel is the fulfillment and perfection of the old message. *For what the law* (the Old Covenant or old message) *was powerless to do because it was weakened by the flesh, God did by sending his own Son* (the New Covenant, the Gospel).... (8:3). Through every reference to the Old Testament in this book, Paul strengthened the power of the Gospel he was appointed to preach and teach.

Draw a square around the phrase **Jesus Christ our Lord** *(4). Now put a square around* **descendant of David** *(3),* **Spirit of holiness** *(4) and* **Son of God** *(4). Underline the phrases* **regarding His Son** *(3) and* **through him we received grace and apostleship** *(5).*

Jesus Christ

We are all impressed when we think of the apostle Paul. His influence, his faith, his travels, his sacrifice, and his writings inspire us. If he were the only one we were going to encounter on this walk, it would be worth the journey. We are going to walk through Romans with the Apostle Paul! However, in the introduction to Romans, Paul is just the opening act. He only mentioned himself to establish his authority to talk about the main act, Jesus Christ our Lord (1:3-4).

So much will be revealed and taught about Jesus through the book that we only get a brief preview here in the introduction. He is the Grace of God personified that fulfills the law and ushers in the Gospel that offers us the gift of righteousness. The Gospel is all about Him; He is the good news! He is also linked to the Old Covenant, being a direct descendant of King David, the greatest King of Israel. This also speaks to the humanity of Christ. He was born, and he had human ancestry and human DNA. But He was not only human, He was also divine (God). He was indwelled by the Spirit of holiness (the Holy Spirit) and constantly connected to the Father every moment of His earthly existence until He was separated on the cross to bear our sin. These two things mean that He is 100% human and 100% divine. His humanity was necessary in order for Him to identify with our condition and in order for Him to experience death for us. His divinity was necessary to accomplish His sinless perfection and ability to carry the sins of the world. Later, Paul will call Jesus the *second Adam* (Romans 5). The first Adam brought unrighteousness into the world, and the second Adam brings righteousness. Paul wanted to be connected to Jesus so he shared that the grace and apostleship he received came through Jesus. He was not just a messenger of the Gospel; He was Jesus' messenger.

---

*Highlight the phrase **all in Rome** (7). Now highlight **called to belong to Jesus Christ** (6), **loved by God** (7) and **called to be saints** (7).*

The Church at Rome

Finally, we meet the Roman believers. Paul explained in verse 5 that his purpose was specifically to call people from among the Gentiles to the *obedience that comes from faith*. Then in verse 6, he affirmed that the believers at Rome were among those who had been called to that obedience and now belonged to Christ. There is no clear historical evidence concerning the origin of this church. Rome, of course, was the center of the Empire and the destination for many travellers. It is possible that some who heard the teachings of Jesus Himself travelled to Rome and shared their faith. Perhaps someone who had been in Jerusalem on the day of Pentecost returned to Rome filled with the Spirit and testified. The early dispersion of Christians from Jerusalem could also have resulted in converts in Rome. In any case, by the time Paul wrote this letter, the church was thriving and their reputation was widely known (1:8). It seems from the references throughout the book that there were both Jewish and Gentile believers in the church at Rome. The majority, it seems, were Gentile (1:5).

This church was part of a larger group of Gentiles that had been called to the *obedience that comes from faith*. In verse 1 Paul stated that he was *called*, now this same Greek word is used of the Roman believers. They did not initiate this relationship; they were invited into it by God Himself. The relationship would not be the same as the one offered under the Old Covenant. The obedience required by the Old Covenant focused on doing what the law required, but the obedience of the New Covenant is simply believing (faith). We will not be justified or declared righteous by doing but by believing.

Paul affirmed that these believers belonged to Jesus, were loved by God, and had been invited to be saints. This was not a reference to the position of sainthood that is bestowed upon specific believers because of their piety. It is our identity as those who have been called out from the world and set apart to be His people. They were also being offered grace and peace from the Father and from the Son. This part of the introduction would certainly have been an encouragement to the church as they read the letter. These facts were not true because they were keeping the commandments, but because they were obedient to believe the Gospel. By God's grace through their faith, they were declared to be who Paul then affirmed them to be.

What was true of the Roman believers is true of us. We could change the opening phrase of verse 7 by writing *to all in* _____ placing our location in the blank. If we are followers of Christ, we did not earn our position, we were invited into it graciously by God Himself. Not only that, but we are also loved and called to be saints, set apart as a special treasure for God.

We have now met our travelling companions on this trail through Romans. We will walk together with the Apostle Paul, Jesus Christ, and other believers who have been invited into relationship with God through the Gospel.

Questions to Ponder:

1. Do any of the words used to describe Paul also describe you? If so, which ones and in what ways do they describe you?

2. Who is walking with you on your journey of faith?

3. How important is God's invitation to this journey?

Day 3

♦♦♦♦♦♦♦♦♦♦♦♦♦♦♦♦♦♦♦♦♦♦

Making Connections
(*Romans 1:8-15*)

8 First, I thank my God through Jesus Christ for all of you, because your faith is being reported all over the world. 9 God, whom I serve with my whole heart in preaching the gospel of his Son, is my witness how constantly I remember you 10 in my prayers at all times; and I pray that now at last by God's will the way may be opened for me to come to you. 11 I long to see you so that I may impart to you some spiritual gift to make you strong— 12 that is, that you and I may be mutually encouraged by each other's faith. 13 I do not want you to be unaware, brothers and sisters, that I planned many times to come to you (but have been prevented from doing so until now) in order that I might have a harvest among you, just as I have had among the other Gentiles. 14 I am obligated both to Greeks and non-Greeks, both to the wise and the foolish. 15 That is why I am so eager to preach the gospel also to you who are in Rome. 16 For I am not ashamed of the gospel, because it is the power of God for the salvation of everyone who believes: first for the Jew, then for the Gentile. 17 For in the gospel the righteousness from God is revealed—a righteousness that is by faith from first to last, just as it is written: "The righteous will live by faith."

Years ago I went with a tour group to the Holy Land. On the night of our arrival in Jerusalem, we were given an itinerary and map to outline our travels. I remember looking over the information that night in my hotel room with excitement, eagerly anticipating specific stops along the way. The next morning our tour bus pulled up in front of the hotel and we all got on, maps in hand, expectancy and excitement in the air. We were all ready to get moving on this tour! However, before the bus pulled out into Jerusalem traffic, the tour guide spent about 15 minutes getting to know us, telling us about himself and then giving us an overview of the trip and sharing his desire for us on this tour. He communicated that he wanted us to experience the Holy Land personally, not just see it. Each day of the trip he would encourage us before we got off of the bus in Bethlehem or beside the Sea of Galilee to personally insert ourselves into the story and experience it.

As we take our stroll through the book of Romans, imagine the Apostle Paul, taking a few minutes before we head up the trail, to share with us in a similar manner. First Paul pauses to let these Roman believers hear his heart for them and for this journey they will make together (1:8-15). After he expresses his love, gratitude and prayers for them, he shares what he truly desires for them (1:16-17).

We may be eager to get on with the journey, but the few moments we will spend here before we actually begin will be invaluable in helping us get the most out of our experience.

> *Circle **I thank my God** (8) and **your faith** (8) and draw a line connecting them. Circle **I pray** (10) and **the way may be opened for me to come to you** (10) and draw a line connecting them. Put a square around **so that** (11), **that is** (12) and **in order that** (13). Underline **impart to you some spiritual gift** (11) and put a number one in front of it. Underline **have a harvest among you** (13) and put a number two in front of it. Underline **eager to preach the gospel** (15) and put a number three in front of it.*

Paul's Heart for the Roman Christians

Paul begins this section by expressing his deep gratitude for the Roman church. This is a great way to begin since everyone loves to be appreciated! Paul was thankful, not for some great act of service, some generous gift to the needy, or some beautiful building project they had completed. He was thankful for their faith. Remember that this was what he was called to invite others into, "the obedience that comes from faith" (1:5). Their faith was surely manifested in specific acts of obedience that had attracted the attention of people all over the Empire but Paul was more thankful for the faith that prompted those actions. Paul knew that faith reproduces itself. He fully expected that the testimony of their faith would prompt faith in others. James 2 teaches us "faith without works is dead". Our works and our actions are the tangible, visible evidences of our faith. Because of this it is easy for us to focus on the outward works and fail to cultivate the inward faith. Paul's comment shows that if faith is present, cultivated and growing, appropriate works and behaviors will not be an issue. Note also that Paul is grateful for their faith even though he personally was not the one to share the gospel with them. Paul was truly devoted to the gospel and not just **his** ministry. So much more could be accomplished for the Kingdom of God if we all adopted this mentality and worked together, rejoicing in each other's victories and supporting each other during times of difficulty.

Paul's care for these believers extended beyond just being thankful for their faith. He desired their greater good so he offered up "constant" prayers for them (1:9-10). He not only prayed for them but he specifically prayed that he could come and visit them (1:10). The language Paul uses as he expresses his desire to visit Rome gives us an insight into his dependence on God. Paul did not call the shots, God did. Paul did not always know what God was doing or where God would lead him next. He had made many plans to visit Rome but on each occasion his plan was hindered or thwarted (1:13). He prays that it might be God's will for him to go to Rome (1:10) and closes out the book by expressing that this has been his desire for many years (15:23). Paul was dependent on God for direction and open doors. His faith was in God alone, not in any plan that he might make. He did not "make things happen" but joined God in what He was doing.

Paul's desire to visit Rome was motivated by more than his

gratefulness for their testimony and his ongoing prayers for them. He was also not motivated by seeing the sights of Rome or hobnobbing with Roman officials. The motivation for his desire was three-fold and is indicated by the words "so that" in 1:11. He expresses that he wanted to visit them "so that" he might impart a spiritual gift to them (1:11), reap a harvest of fruit among them (1:13) and fulfill his obligation to preach the gospel to them (1:14).

There are many examples of the apostles visiting various churches and groups of believers and imparting or sharing spiritual gifts with them. In Acts 8 Phillip the evangelist had shared the gospel with Samaria but it wasn't until the arrival of the apostles Peter and John that the gift of the Spirit was given to them. In Acts 19 Paul meets up with a group of believers who had not yet received the gift of the Spirit. He lays hands on them and they receive the gift, speaking in tongues and prophesying (Acts 19:6). So our first thought when Paul says he wants to visit them to impart a gift is that perhaps these believers had not received the gift of the Holy Spirit because they had not yet been visited by an apostle. However, Paul clarifies the gift when he says "that is" the encouragement that comes from the mutual sharing of faith (1:12). The gift of the Spirit having already been received, both Paul and the Roman believers could share from the Spirit and benefit from this gift. The purpose of the sharing of this gift was to encourage and to strengthen (1:11,12). When spirit-filled believers interact with each other, a mutual gift is exchanged between them that both encourages and strengthens. We can experience this every time we meet together with other believers. There is a bond, a connection and a common thread that resonates in us and communicates that we are a part of something that is much bigger than ourselves. I have experienced this with the Zulu people of South Africa, the Slavic people of Romania and the Latin cultures of South America even when I didn't understand a word that was being said. This connection is a living connection, Spirit to Spirit. For this reason, isolation is detrimental to the believer and a desire and eagerness to be together is natural. This explains Paul's great desire to visit Rome. The "harvest" (1:13) that he hoped to reap among them is a reference to the fruit that would be borne by their mutual sharing of faith. The fruit of ministry is not just the people that come to faith but the experiences of faith we share together.

Having made a personal connection with these believers by expressing his gratitude and desire for relationship, Paul now shares his internal motivation. The Apostle has an inner compulsion to preach the gospel (1:15). This compulsion was not out of duty or driven by guilt. It was a compulsion that came from his constant awareness that the way to God had been accomplished and was available to all by grace through faith and that he had personally experienced the life and righteousness that comes by faith in the Gospel. Because of the price God paid for this good news and the personal way in which He shared it with Paul himself, Paul felt indebted to share it with every race (Greek and non-Greek) and every personality (wise and unwise). Imagine being exposed to a complete cure for cancer. Having applied and experienced complete healing through this cure, the compulsion to share it with everyone else who was struggling with cancer would be overwhelming. Sharing the gospel was not a duty or obligation for Paul, it was a passionate response to his own experience. Paul wasn't saying that above all people, he wanted to see the Romans the most. He was saying that his desire to share the gospel with all people, included sharing it with the Romans (1:15). The compulsion is further emphasized by the fact that Paul was eager (1:15) or ready and willing to preach the gospel to them.

So Paul, our trail leader, has connected with us by sharing his heart for us. Now he is ready to give us the overall purpose of our experience with him on this walk.

Highlight **gospel** *(16),* ***power of God*** *(16) and* ***a righteousness that is by faith*** *(17).*

The Heart of Paul's Message

At the very heart of Paul's message to the church at Rome is the gospel. He had already told them that this is what he was called to

(1:1,2). While the declaration of this gospel may appear foolish to the world (I Corinthians 1:18), Paul was not afraid to travel the world boldly proclaiming it. He was not ashamed because the gospel is the power of God for the salvation of everyone who believes. The word for power in 1:16 is the Greek word *dunamis* which means the ability to accomplish something.

The gospel (Christ died, was buried and rose again for the forgiveness of sin) is extended to us by God's grace. Our personal choice of faith in receiving the gospel releases the power of the gospel in us, delivering us from sin; from the mastery of sin (6:14), from the wages of sin (6:23) and from the condemnation of sin (8:1). This power to save is unleashed for everyone who believes and accomplishes salvation or complete deliverance in us. Again, as Paul introduced in 1:5, obeying the gospel is not about conduct, not about adherence to the law, it is about believing. It requires no work on our part because the work was completed by Christ. This gospel is available to all. The Jews were offered the gospel first (with reference to chronology) and then the Gentiles. Teaching that we must give special priority to reaching the Jewish people with the gospel contradicts Paul's teaching throughout this book (3:9,22,29).

It certainly is freeing to know that the power required for ministry does not come from us; from our gifting, from our strength or from our efforts. The gospel itself, already accomplished, is the power required to save a soul and change a life and it is available to everyone who will believe.

In verse 17 we finally get our first sighting of righteousness. Recall from the introduction that righteousness is "being as one ought to be" or "as one was meant to be". It is the life God always meant for us to live. Before Christ, the Jewish people were in a covenant relationship with God. They entered the covenant when Moses received the Ten Commandments and the law at Mt. Sinai (Exodus 19-20) so it is sometimes referred to as the Mosaic Covenant or the Old Covenant. Since God is righteous, His people must be righteous in order to be in relationship with Him. The law that God gave to Moses was God's righteous standard. In order to experience the life God always intended, we must live up to God's standard. If a person could keep the whole law, they would be declared righteous (justified) and would be "as they were meant to be". Throughout the book of Romans, Paul makes it clear that apart from God there is no one who is righteous (3:10). He also states that it is impossible for anyone to be declared righteous by the law (3:20). The Old Covenant left everyone striving, guilty, unrighteous and falling short (3:23).

Jesus came to establish a New Covenant. He was born of a virgin so he did not inherit the sinful nature that had been passed down through Adam. He lived a sinless life and so satisfied the requirements of God's righteous law. Then, in spite of the fact that he was undeserving of death, He died as a substitute for us, taking our sin upon himself and, in exchange, giving us His righteousness. This righteousness is "by faith" and not "by law". This righteousness is His righteousness and not dependent on us so it will endure until we are presented whole to the righteous judge (by faith from first to last 1:17). This righteousness of the New Covenant, like the gospel itself (1:2) was prophesied in the Old Testament through the prophet Habakkuk (Habakkuk 2:4). It was hidden from those under the law but is now shown (1:17) by the gospel. In his other epistles Paul refers to this as the mystery that has now been revealed. The mystery is the gift of righteousness to the Gentiles (Ephesians 3:6) and is further defined as "Christ in you, the hope of glory" (Colossians 1:27). This paradigm shattering revelation has continually had aftershocks hundreds of years later. This very concept and Scripture was instrumental in Martin Luther's turn from obedience to faith which sparked the Protestant Reformation. It is also this truth that is fueling a resurgence of the doctrine of grace and the exchanged life (Galatians 2:20) that is taking place in the 21st century.

This is where the guide (Paul) who is leading us through this book pauses to alert us to his greatest desire. He doesn't want us just to know about this righteousness, understand this righteousness or even receive this righteousness. Paul desires that we learn to live in this righteousness, to experience the life God always intended us to live, completely accepted by God, and to realize that it cannot be purchased, earned or deserved. It is a free gift.

Questions to Ponder:

1. How can you make this study more of an experience and less like mere education?

2. For what was Paul expressing thankfulness in regards to the Romans? What was he anticipating experiencing with them when he visited? Why is this so important?

3. What can we learn about making plans from Paul's desire to visit Rome?

4. What was the main focus of Paul's ministry?

5. What is God's desire for us in reference to righteousness?

Day 4

♦♦♦♦♦♦♦♦♦♦♦♦♦♦♦♦♦♦♦♦♦♦♦♦

A Stark Contrast
(Romans 1:18-32)

18 The wrath of God is being revealed from heaven against all the godlessness and wickedness of people, who suppress the truth by their wickedness, 19 since what may be known about God is plain to them, because God has made it plain to them. 20 For since the creation of the world God's invisible qualities—his eternal power and divine nature—have been clearly seen, being understood from what has been made, so that people are without excuse. 21 For although they knew God, they neither glorified him as God nor gave thanks to him, but their thinking became futile and their foolish hearts were darkened. 22 Although they claimed to be wise, they became fools 23 and exchanged the glory of the immortal God for images made to look like a mortal human being and birds and animals and reptiles. 24 Therefore God gave them over in the sinful desires of their hearts to sexual impurity for the degrading of their bodies with one another. 25 They exchanged the truth of God for a lie, and worshiped and served created things rather than the Creator—who is forever praised. Amen. 26 Because of this, God gave them over to shameful lusts. Even their women exchanged natural sexual relations for unnatural ones. 27 In the same way the men also abandoned natural relations with women and were inflamed with lust for one another. Men committed shameful acts with other men, and received in themselves the due penalty for their error. 28 Furthermore, since they did not think it worthwhile to retain the knowledge of God, so God gave them over to a depraved mind, so that they do what ought not to be done. 29 They have become filled with every kind of wickedness, evil, greed and depravity. They are full of envy, murder, strife, deceit and malice. They are gossips, 30 slanderers, God-haters, insolent, arrogant and boastful; they invent ways of doing evil; they disobey their parents; 31 they are senseless, faithless, heartless, ruthless.

32 Although they know God's righteous decree that those who do such things deserve death, they not only continue to do these very things but also approve of those who practice them.

I remember one time hiking down a forest trail, enjoying the shade of the trees, drinking in the lush green life all around me. All of a sudden I stepped out of the trees and into an open area that provided no shade, very little green, and smelled of stagnant water. Wetlands. Swamp. The contrast between the forest and the swamp was so stark, I turned around to make sure I hadn't gotten off of the path!

As we step from Romans 1:17 to Romans 1:18, we feel the same stark contrast. We end verse 17 with the fruit of the Gospel, righteousness, living life as it was always meant to be. Then in verse 18, we are immediately introduced to the concept of God's wrath! Don't worry, we are still on the right path, but we are not staying here, just passing through and observing.

---

*Draw a box around the word **wrath** (18). Draw a line from the word wrath to the word **godlessness** and the word **wickedness**. Highlight the phrase **suppress the truth** (18) and **so that people are without excuse** (20).*

The Wrath of God

The word used for wrath here is also used for the punishment that flows out of wrath. The word is used 12 times in Romans and is always connected with God's judgment of sin (3:5, 12:19). The object of God's wrath is the godlessness (lack of reverence toward God) and the wickedness (a violation of righteousness) of humanity. Remember that God's righteous standard had been communicated to his people through the Ten Commandments. In direct violation of the first four commandments the world has a total disregard for God that has led them into idolatry (godlessness). In direct violation of the last four commandments the world has chosen immoral behavior (wickedness). God is righteous and must judge these violations of righteousness by the law of sin and death; for the wages of sin is death (Romans 3:23, 8:2). The rest of this passage chronicles man's descent into idolatry and immorality, deserving of God's wrath.

Why are we talking about wrath? In Romans 1:14-17, we were introduced to a righteousness revealed to us by the Gospel and available to us by faith. If we were talking about a cure for cancer, we would want to take the message to everyone who had cancer. They would be our target audience. But we are talking about the problem of unrighteousness so we need to take the message to all who are unrighteous. Beginning now in verse 18, we are seeing the universal need for that gospel because the entire human race is ungodly and unrighteous, deserving of the angry judgment of a righteous God. The presentation of the Gospel must begin with the need for the gospel which is evidenced by the sinfulness of man and this sinfulness is universal. We highlighted the phrase *so that people are without excuse* in 1:19. This phrase appears again in 2:1. It has always been the case that people categorize sin and indict others as guiltier or more deserving of God's wrath than themselves. Paul concludes in this passage that we are all equally guilty because mankind has willfully suppressed (1:18) the truth about His power and divine nature (Godhead) that is so clearly demonstrated in both the act of creation and the creation itself (1:19-20). The judgment of God rightly falls on the world, so we all need Jesus.

The wickedness of humanity that starts with a total disregard for God (suppressing the truth) begins a slide down a slippery slope toward destruction. Disregard for God is first evidenced by refusal to acknowledge Him or express gratitude toward Him (1:21). Ignoring God begins to affect man's thinking which becomes futile (empty or vain) and their hearts are darkened (unable to express or receive love). This mental ignorance and emotional disconnect leads to a series of actions and reactions in man's relationship with God.

> *Circle the word **exchanged** in 1:23 and the phrase **God gave them over** in verse 24. Draw a line between these two circles and write the word **so** on the line.*

The First Exchange

When children are caught in a fight, their first response is usually to point to the other and say "he started it." In humanity's fall from God, it is important to note that man started it.

We have already seen that man's mental and emotional state was adversely affected by the decision to ignore God. In this state they make a decision to exchange (trade one thing for another) the glory (splendor, recognition) of God for that of images or visual representations of God's creation in the animal world. In other words they made physical, tangible depictions of God (idols) and worshipped them. This is a direct violation of the second commandment which states *You shall not make for yourself an image in the form of anything in heaven above or on the earth beneath or in the waters below. You shall not bow down to them or worship them...* (Exodus 20:4,5). Mankind didn't start by actually worshiping a rock, a tree, or a statue. First they made images to represent God and ascribed the glory that was due God to the image. This is exactly what Israel did at the foot of Mt. Sinai when they made the golden calf and worshipped it. Exodus 32 says that Aaron built an altar in front of the calf and proclaimed a feast to Jehovah. They wanted something physical and tangible that they could attach to because they had rejected the spiritual presence and authority of God. Their rejection of God had progressed from passive (not glorifying or thanking) to active (giving something else the glory due to Him). Whenever we give more glory, honor or attention to something physical (food, person, church, football team, fashion, etc.,) than we do to God, we are guilty of idolatry. We are giving glory to things God has given us rather than giving glory to God Himself.

As a result of the progression of their rejection, God made a judicial decision to give them over to their sinful desires (1:24).

God hands mankind over to the downward spiral of his own desire. The relational emptiness that results from abandoning God naturally leads to sexual impurity (1:24). Mankind replaces God with an image and then replaces the spiritual intimacy of relationship with God with the physical intimacy of sexual acts. Idolatry leads to immorality and then both this ungodliness and unrighteousness trigger the wrath of God (1:18). God didn't choose for them to move in this direction, nor did he cause it to happen. He simply allowed them to be ruled by their own wills.

Circle the word **exchanged** *in 1:25. Now circle the phrase* **God gave them over** *in 1:26. Draw a line between these two and write the word* **so** *on the line.*

The Second Exchange

This second exchange involves mankind's violation of the first commandment that reads, *You shall have no other gods before me* (Exodus 20:3). They now exchange (trade one thing for another) the true God for the false gods they themselves have created. No longer do the images represent God in a tangible form, they have actually become their gods.

As a result of their further rejection of God, God allows their drift into immorality to cross the lines of gender. The homosexual acts of men and women described in 1:26-27 are not being portrayed as the worst sins mankind could commit, but are simply part of the downward spiral that naturally occurs when man rejects the spiritual and sinks into the sensual. In the first exchange, they were degrading or dishonoring their bodies through immoral acts (1:24) and now they are guilty of perversion or wandering from the intended creative order.

This mention of homosexuality is rare. It represents a diversion or a perversion of God's creative order (created them male and female). If we reject God as creator it is logical that we will eventually reject God's creative order. Man's dominion over the earth, care of the planet, rhythm of work and rest, creation of male and female to become one, etc., were all part of that order. As mankind rejects God it degenerates into a rejection of this order. Just as in any other sin, we will not persuade the world to accept God's creative order until they accept the God of creation. The answer to the problem of homosexuality, like any other sin, is the Gospel.

---

*Highlight the phrase **they did not think it worthwhile to retain the knowledge of God** in 1:28. Highlight the phrase **he gave them over** in 1:28. Draw a line between the two phrases and write the word **so** on the line.*

The Third Exchange

While Paul doesn't repeat the use of the word "exchange" here, he does repeat the phrase "he gave them over." They had exchanged the spiritual for the physical (1:21-24), exchanged relationship with God for sexual immorality (1:25-27), and were completely rejecting the very concept of God, considering God to be irrelevant and useless to their every day lives. God allowed the very depravity of their nature to reveal their depraved or reprobate mind. This word "depraved" literally describes something that has been unapproved or unacceptable. Righteousness is that which is acceptable, that which is as it ought to be. A reprobate mind, according to 1:28 does, *what ought not to be done*.

This final dive into depravity is described by a long list of wickedness in 1:29-31. This list includes such things as gossip, malice, arrogance, and disobedience to parents. It ends with the qualities of being senseless, faithless, heartless, and ruthless. While the preacher may want to point to homosexuality as the bottom of the barrel, Paul takes us deeper into these sins that often are less demonstrative but deeply motivate wicked actions. These last four words all begin with the Greek prefix a- which literally means "without." Mankind's final indictment is that they are without sense, without faith, without heart, and without pity. We should not be surprised by the dominant presence of these qualities in society but we must be careful that we don't let them creep into our lives as followers of Christ.

Paul took their wickedness and compared it to the righteous decree of God (the law). The obvious conclusion is that the flagrant disregard for God's righteous standard condemns them to death (the law of sin and death). This knowledge not only didn't stop them from continuing in their sin, they moved from participants in wickedness to encouraging and promoting wickedness in others. Paul actually ended this passage with the opening phrase of 2:1, *You therefore, have no excuse*. The human race is guilty of ungodliness and unrighteousness, deserving of the wrath of God and desperately in need of God's righteousness available by faith in the gospel.

Summary of the Downward Spiral of Mankind

1. Suppress the truth about God that is evidence in Creation.
2. Disregard God in everyday life (refuse to acknowledge or thank)
3. Man's thinking becomes empty and heart darkens (inability to give and receive love).
4. First exchange
   - trade glory of God for an image of God
   - violates the 1st commandment
   - mankind is given over to the sinful desire
   - relational emptiness seeks solace in sexual intimacy/impurity
5. Second Exchange
   - trade glory of God for something that is not God at all
   - violates the 2nd commandment
   - sexual impurity increases, rejecting God's creative order (homosexuality)
6. Third exchange
   - completely reject the concept of God
   - senseless, faithless, heartless, ruthless
7. Participation in evil turns to promotion of evil

Questions to Ponder:

1. What is Paul's purpose in this passage? Is he teaching a
      hierarchy of sin?

2. List the three exchanges mentioned in this passage. What
      are some examples in our own culture that this is
      happening?

3. Where does this downward spiral end?

4. In light of what Paul is teaching in this passage, what is the
      answer for the ungodliness and wickedness in the world?

Day 5

◆◆◆◆◆◆◆◆◆◆◆◆◆◆◆◆◆◆◆◆◆◆◆◆

God's Righteous Judgment
(Romans 2:1-16)

You, therefore, have no excuse, you who pass judgment on someone else, for at whatever point you judge the other, you are condemning yourself, because you who pass judgment do the same things. 2 Now we know that God's judgment against those who do such things is based on truth. 3 So when you, a mere man, pass judgment on them and yet do the same things, do you think you will escape God's judgment? 4 Or do you show contempt for the riches of his kindness, tolerance and patience, not realizing that God's kindness leads you toward repentance? 5 But because of your stubbornness and your unrepentant heart, you are storing up wrath against yourself for the day of God's wrath, when his righteous judgment will be revealed. 6 God "will give to each person according to what he has done." 7 To those who by persistence in doing good seek glory, honor and immortality, he will give eternal life. 8 But for those who are self-seeking and who reject the truth and follow evil, there will be wrath and anger. 9 There will be trouble and distress for every human being who does evil: first for the Jew, then for the Gentile; 10 but glory, honor and peace for everyone who does good: first for the Jew, then for the Gentile. 11 For God does not show favoritism. 12 All who sin apart from the law will also perish apart from the law, and all who sin under the law will be judged by the law. 13 For it is not those who hear the law who are righteous in God's sight, but it is those who obey the law who will be declared righteous. 14 (Indeed, when Gentiles, who do not have the law, do by nature things required by the law, they are a law for themselves, even though they do not have the law. 15 Since they show that the requirements of the law are written on their hearts, their consciences also bearing witness, and their thoughts now accusing, now even defending them.) 16 This will take place on the day when God judges people's secrets through Jesus Christ, as my gospel declares.

Sometimes on a nature trail, even the most inexperienced outdoorsman can make an accurate observation. If you are walking along the trail and suddenly are overcome by the distinct smell of pine and then, as you look around, you see an abundance of evergreen trees with pine cones, you could amaze your fellow hikers by announcing, "I think we are in a pine grove!" As we walk down through the first half of Romans 2, even the casual reader can pick up on the repetition of the subject of judgment that is the focus of this passage.

Circle every occurrence of the word judge or judgment in 2:1-16 (you should end up with 9 circles). Now make a square around every occurrence of the word wrath (you should end up with 3 squares).

Paul's passionate speech about the ungodliness and wickedness of humanity probably had the readers in a frenzy of shouting "Amen" by the end of Romans 1. They agreed with Paul that "those heathen" were so ungodly. Haven't you been in a church service where the topic was about the ungodliness of the world system, the liberal politicians, the immoral or the terrorists? Christians love to shout "Amen" and get passionate when they are talking about someone else's sin. Paul began in Romans 1:18 stating that God's wrath is being revealed against that ungodliness and wickedness. God's wrath is His judgment (hence the connection between the two words in this passage). The Greek word that is translated judge or judgment in this passage is *krino*. It means "to pronounce judgment as to whether something is right or wrong." It conjures up a picture of the judge sitting at the front of the courtroom bringing down the gavel on the desk and saying "guilty". This particular word, though, is even broader than that and includes not just the pronouncement but also the sentencing; "guilty and sentenced to 30 days in jail". In verse 1, the word is linked to the word condemn and so carries the broader meaning of not just the judgment but the punishment as well. The frenzy of "Amen" shouting faded quickly into silence as the reader began to realize Paul was also talking about them.

No Excuse

The long list of ungodliness and unrighteousness in chapter 1 ends with the conclusion that everyone is without excuse (2:1). While the Jewish people were not specifically being singled out at the beginning of chapter 2 (that doesn't happen until verse 17) Paul was talking about them in general terms when he addressed those who were judging others in verse 1. Evidently, there was a group of people that were busy pointing the finger at others (or shouting Amen!) while they themselves were guilty of some of the same things. Paul's conclusion was that those who pointed the finger at others were actually condemning themselves as well (remember when you point one finger at another, three of your fingers are pointing back at yourself). The Jewish people believed in the judgment of God but held the opinion that because of their status as God's chosen people and because of the covenant God had made with them, they would be exempt from the judgment. Somehow this had translated into a freedom to judge others. But God's judgment is based on truth (2:2) and not on position or ancestry. Those who condemn others will definitely not escape God's judgment (2:3). In fact, the goodness of God that He has shown to the Jewish people through the Old Covenant was not meant to exclude them from judgment but was actually a means to bring them to see their need for repentance (2:4).

---

*Highlight the words **righteous judgment** in 2:5. Now underline the words **each person** in 2:6, **every human being** in 2:9, **first for the Jew, then for the Greek** in 2:9 and **all** in 2:12. Draw a line from **righteous judgment** to all of these words.*

The Jewish people, though, had not repented but had stubbornly trusted in their status. As a result, they were actually piling up wrath or judgment for their godlessness and wickedness that would all catch up with them when God's *righteous judgment* was revealed (2:5). The Greek word used here is *dikaiokrisia*. This word is a combination of the word for righteous and the word for judgment (the only use of this word in the New Testament). It is perfect judgment, just judgment and irrefutable judgment. It is linked to the word wrath in 2:5 and thus is part of the wrath that will be revealed against godlessness and wickedness in 1:18. Paul has set the stage to introduce the main point of this passage. Everyone will be judged. The wrath of God that is being revealed from heaven is for *each person* (2:6), *every human being* (2:9), *first for the Jew, then for the Gentile* (2:9) and for *all* (2:12). Because the problem of godlessness and wickedness is universal, the judgment of God will also be universal.

> *Underline **condemning yourself** in 2:1, **based on truth** in 2:2, **God's kindness leads you toward repentance** in 2:4 and **God will give to each person according to what he has done** in 2:6.*

The Law Game

What will be the standard of this universal judgment? It is a righteous judgment (2:5) so the standard must be righteousness, which according to the Jews, was the law of God. If the Jews wanted to claim their special status, they would also have to accept that their judgment would be carried out under the law of the Old Covenant. The law could declare someone righteous if they lived up to the standard of righteousness the law represented. So, Paul says that everyone will be given (judgment) according to what he has done (2:6). Those who do good will get eternal life (2:7) and those who do evil will get wrath (2:8) both for the Jew and the Gentile (2:9). This sounds a lot like works salvation and has been used to teach against the doctrine of grace. Remember, though, that Paul is speaking in the context of the law. If someone could do good (obey the whole law) they would earn eternal life, but the truth is *there is no one who does good, no not one* (3:11) which is why *no one will be declared righteous in his sight by observing the law* (3:20). Paul was using the Jew's favored position to pull the rug out from under them and show them that they were all deserving of God's wrath and in need of the Gospel. Taken out of context this passage seems to indicate that we will be judged according to our works but the truth is Paul is teaching just the opposite. Our works condemn us, all of us.

The truth is that sin under the law (Jews) and sin apart from the law (Gentiles) is all considered godless and wicked and will be judged. The Gentiles may not have had the written law, but they had the moral code written on their hearts from the creation so that they knew right from wrong (2:12-15). So the judgment will be universal and will include even those things kept secret from others. This judgment will be carried out by Jesus Christ. Christ took upon Himself all of our sin on the cross. God looked upon that sin and judged it by the law of sin and death; the wages of sin is death. God pronounced Jesus guilty and sentenced him to death (judged Him). Therefore I will NOT be judged by my works because Jesus took that judgment for me on the cross. Those who have received this gift by faith will stand before God clothed in the righteousness of Christ. Those who don't receive this gift will stand before Him as the final judge because the Father has entrusted all judgment to the Son (John 5:22).

Dr. Andrew Farley likes to say that if you play the "law" game, you will lose. There are those who preach and teach that our works play a role in our salvation or our standing before God. In Romans 2 Paul went along with those who believed this way. In a sense he pretended to play the "law" game with them for a while, but showed them that it all ends in judgment. Others focused on preaching judgment as a way to motivate people toward repentance. Paul made it clear in this passage that it isn't the fear of judgment that leads people to repentance, it is the goodness (grace and love) of God (2:4). The Gospel is good news. It is not "you can escape judgment," it is "you are loved and forgiven", because I took your judgment. Since the law game doesn't work, beware of teaching that promotes striving to please God or teaching that promotes a hierarchy of believers that is based on behavior. Because all sin was judged on the cross, we stand at the foot of the cross on level ground.

Paul was "playing the law game" with them to bring them to a conclusion. He was showing them that by using the law against others, they were actually condemning themselves (2:1) because God's judgment is based on His righteous truth (2:2). Any kindness or mercy that God may have shown to them does not negate God's judgment, but is designed to draw them to conclude that they are guilty and need to repent (2:4). The bottom line of judgment by the law is that each person, regardless of their position, profession, heritage or rank, will be judged based on how their works stack up to the righteous law of God (2:6). The conclusion, as we will see in the latter part of this chapter is that we are all... GUILTY!

Questions to Ponder:

1. Imagine you are in the Heavenly Courtroom standing before God the righteous judge. As the gavel falls and judgment is pronounced, what will He say about you?

2. Some people say that the God of the Old Covenant was angry, vengeful and jealous and the God of the New Covenant is gracious, loving and forgiving. Since we know God based on what you learned in this lesson?

3. Which is a better motivator toward holy living, grace or law? Why?

Day 6

♦♦♦♦♦♦♦♦♦♦♦♦♦♦♦♦♦♦♦♦♦♦♦♦♦

How about those Jews?
(Romans 2:17-29)

17 Now you, if you call yourself a Jew; if you rely on the law and boast in God; 18 if you know his will and approve of what is superior because you are instructed by the law; 19 if you are convinced that you are a guide for the blind, a light for those who are in the dark, 20 an instructor of the foolish, a teacher of little children, because you have in the law the embodiment of knowledge and truth— 21 you, then, who teach others, do you not teach yourself? You who preach against stealing, do you steal? 22 You who say that people should not commit adultery, do you commit adultery? You who abhor idols, do you rob temples? 23 You who boast in the law, do you dishonor God by breaking the law? 24 As it is written: "God's name is blasphemed among the Gentiles because of you." 25 Circumcision has value if you observe the law, but if you break the law, you have become as though you had not been circumcised. 26 So then, if those who are not circumcised keep the law's requirements, will they not be regarded as though they were circumcised? 27 The one who is not circumcised physically and yet obeys the law will condemn you who, even though you have the written code and circumcision, are a lawbreaker. 28 A person is not a Jew who is one only outwardly, nor is circumcision merely outward and physical. 29 No, a person is a Jew who is one inwardly; and circumcision is circumcision of the heart, by the Spirit, not by the written code. Such a person's praise is not from other people, but from God.

If you have ever been on a hike with a group, you quickly learn that there are the hikers and the non-hikers. The people who are physically fit, have all of the right gear and know how to pace themselves on a trail, quickly emerge as superior in this environment. Those who are a little out of shape (although round is a shape), wearing flip-flops and have no water bottle quickly lag behind and an "us versus them" spirit quickly arises. Years ago I went on a hike in the Rocky Mountains while attending a retreat. I was quickly made aware of my condition. The higher altitude and my inexperience were resulting in a very slow pace. I had to keep stopping to breathe! As the more experienced hikers continued to pass me, I became more and more aware of my weakness in this area.

What is true in hiking is also true in religious circles. Those who know their Bible, the lyrics to the songs, the religious jargon, and are in positions of leadership in the church often distance themselves from the common folk and begin to develop an air of superiority. Evidently this was happening in the church at Rome and happened to be falling out along the lines of Jews and non-Jews. Having argued the universal guilt of everyone under the law, Paul now turns his attention to those of Jewish heritage.

The theme of the book of Romans was stated in our introduction: I become completely acceptable to God (righteous) by believing (faith) in the sacrifice of Christ for my sin (Gospel) and it is absolutely free (grace). This righteousness that God offers is available to all at no cost to them and is needed by all because of the universal sinfulness of mankind under the law. Therefore we all must approach this gospel from the same point of guilt.

> *Highlight the following words with the same color.* **Jew** *(2:17),* **rely on the law** *(2:17),* **boast** *(2:17),* **superior** *(2:18),* **guide, light** *(2:19) and* **instructor, teacher** *(2:20).* *Now draw a line and connect it to* **you, then** *(2:21)*

What about Those Jews?

But what about those Jews? It is obvious from this passage that the Jewish people in Rome still believed themselves to be superior in some way to the Gentiles. Because they were specifically given the law (the same law that we just learned condemned everyone) and invited into a covenant of law by God, they considered themselves superior and in a position to instruct others in spiritual matters. Paul has been setting them up from the beginning of the book and is now going to lower the truth on them. Let's consider the progression of Paul's thoughts up to this point:

- ☐ The Gospel is the power of God bringing salvation to Jews and Gentiles alike (1:16)
- ☐ The wrath of God is being revealed against *all* godlessness and wickedness (1:18).
- ☐ If you point the finger at others, you also condemn yourselves (2:1).
- ☐ The judgment (wrath) of God will be based on *truth* (2:2), will take into account every man's works (2:6), and will result in death for both those who sin without the law and those who sin under the law (2:12).

Having set the stage, Paul turned his attention toward the Jews (2:17). The Jews were God's chosen people. They had been specifically chosen and invited into a covenant relationship with God under the law. There was a pride associated with being a Jew because of this covenant. They had been entrusted with the law and therefore seemed the best qualified to teach, guide, and instruct others in it. But this attitude missed the point of the covenant and the law. The point was obedience (2:13). Paul began to unravel their superiority by pointing out to them that while condemning others, they were actually condemning themselves. The Jews who were teaching others not to steal, commit adultery, or participate in idolatry were actually just as guilty as those they were teaching. This brought dishonor to God (2:23) and allowed the Gentiles to blaspheme God (2:24).

Now before all of my non-Jewish readers dismiss this passage as inapplicable to them, what if we just changed the language? What if the church members were appointing themselves as teachers, leaders, guides of the unchurched simply because of their position? What if the baptized were bragging about their relationship with God to the unbaptized? Different position but same principle. If we begin to believe that we have something to do with our righteous standing with God, we can begin to think that we are better than others, sit in judgment on others and even condemn others. Remember, it is all God's righteousness and is only available by faith. We have nothing in ourselves to boast about.

---

*Underline **observe the law** (2:25), **keep the law's requirements** (2:26), **obeys the law** (2:27) and circle **circumcision of the heart** (2:29).*

Yeah, But What about Circumcision?

The Jewish nation began in Genesis 12 when God promised to make Abraham a great nation. When Isaac, the promised son was finally born to Abraham and Sarah, God instructed the child to be circumcised. Circumcision was the cutting of the male foreskin and was introduced by God to Abraham as a physical symbol of the covenant He made with Abraham regarding the nation of Israel. Every male child born to a descendant of Abraham (every male Jew) was to be circumcised on the 8th day of life as a symbol that he was a son of the covenant. Later, under the covenant with Moses, those circumcised descendants of Abraham were invited into a special relationship with God based on their obedience to His laws. Circumcision was also a part of this covenant. However, over time, the physical act of circumcision began to be the definition of the covenant itself. Instead of evaluating themselves by whether or not they were obeying the law, they were evaluating themselves by whether or not they were circumcised. Circumcision became the bragging rights of the Jews. In this same way baptism can become synonymous with relationship with God for the "Christian". Trusting in a ritual or outward symbol is not the same as obedience. Under the old covenant it was obedience to the law and under the new covenant it is obedience to the gospel (faith).

So when Paul began to show them that the law actually condemned them, he expected them to ask *what about circumcision*? In the remainder of this chapter, Paul answers this objection (2:25-29). He takes them right back to the point of the covenant relationship. The crux of the covenant wasn't whether or not they were circumcised, but whether or not they obeyed the law (2:13). Circumcision was an outward symbol that a man belonged to God. The only way to really belong to God was to be righteous and righteousness had been defined for them by the law. If someone then, could be righteous by obedience to the law, God would look at him as if he were circumcised because he truly belonged to him. On the contrary, if someone were circumcised but not obeying the law, God would look at him as if he were uncircumcised because he didn't belong to Him. God was concerned with his heart (not his foreskin). Circumcision of the heart was referring to a heart made righteous by obedience to the gospel, not obedience to the law. This righteousness which comes by faith is lived out by the Spirit of God who is in us and not by following a prescribed list of behaviors.

RIGHTEOUS = CIRCUMCISED
UNRIGHTEOUS = UNCIRCUMCISED

THE CONDITION DICTATES THE SYMBOL, THE SYMBOL DOES NOT DICTATE THE CONDITION!

Paul concluded with the reality that those who were circumcised may be able to receive praise from men because of their position, but God would praise those who are righteous. Throughout the epistles of the New Testament the early church was urged to work toward unity. Unity is compromised when a hierarchy of believers emerges because some begin to think of themselves as superior or inferior based upon some action or behavior. Evidently Paul was concerned about the unity of the church at Rome between the Jews and the Gentiles, which is why he was making such a big deal about this issue of circumcision. If righteousness came by the law, there exists a hierarchy of righteousness, some are more righteous and some are less righteous. However, since righteousness is by faith in the Gospel, we are all equally righteous and no hierarchy exists.

Questions to Ponder:

1. What kinds of things did the Jews tend to brag about? How would you relate this problem to our own church culture?

2. For the Jews the outward sign of circumcision had become the very definition of relationship with God. Are there things that we tend to equate with our relationship with God?

3. What was it about being a child of the law that the Jewish people kept leaving out?

4. What is the circumcision of the heart?

Day 7

◆◆◆◆◆◆◆◆◆◆◆◆◆◆◆◆◆◆◆◆◆◆◆◆

Objection!
(Romans 3:1-9)

What advantage, then, is there in being a Jew, or what value is there in circumcision? 2 Much in every way! First of all, the Jews have been entrusted with the very words of God. 3 What if some were unfaithful? Will their unfaithfulness nullify God's faithfulness? 4 Not at all! Let God be true, and every human being a liar. As it is written: "So that you may be proved right when you speak and prevail when you judge." 5 But if our unrighteousness brings out God's righteousness more clearly, what shall we say? That God is unjust in bringing his wrath on us? (I am using a human argument.) 6 Certainly not! If that were so, how could God judge the world? 7 Someone might argue, "If my falsehood enhances God's truthfulness and so increases his glory, why am I still condemned as a sinner?" 8 Why not say—as some slanderously claim that we say— "Let us do evil that good may result"? Their condemnation is just!

We have come to a place on the trail where we must stop and dialogue because someone in the group is not sure they want to continue forward. It's almost like they begin to see where this trail is headed and they are not sure they want to go there. Our guide (Paul) pauses to argue that the objections to moving ahead are unfounded.

I grew up watching detective shows and courtroom drama. *Perry Mason*, *Matlock*, *Barnaby Jones* and *Magnum P.I.* have evolved into *Elementary*, *Law and Order*, and *The Good Wife*. Courtroom drama and the intrigue of investigation capture our attention. We all enjoy the moment when the arguments get heated and the attorney rises to passionately shout, "Objection!"

Paul had been carefully laying down his argument. He asserted that the Gospel is for everyone (1:16), that the whole world is under the righteous judgment of God (1:18), and that even the Jews are not exempt (2:17-29). The Jewish reader had probably followed the argument with a polite nod of the head as he applied it to "those Gentiles." However, as Paul moved toward the end of chapter 2, the Jewish reader became agitated; he could not believe what he was hearing. The words "circumcision has no value" (2:25) brought a look of shock, and by the time Paul closed out this section, the reader was jumping to his feet, "Objection!"

---

*Put a small number one beside the words **what advantage then** (3:1), a small number two beside the words **what if some** (3:3) and a small number three beside the words **but if our** (3:5). Draw a box around the words **much in every way** (3:2), **not at all** (3:4) and **certainly not** (3:6).*

Objection #1: So what is the advantage for the Jewish people?

The Jewish people cherished their position as God's chosen people. They had been called out and set apart for a special covenantal relationship with God. This was a big deal. As Paul developed his argument and preached the universal condemnation of mankind, Jew and Gentile, it became difficult for the Jewish reader to reconcile the status of chosen with this universal concept. The first objection that Paul anticipated was the question, "So what advantage is there in being a Jew?" (3:1). If we are equally condemned with the Gentiles, why be called God's chosen? Paul's response, "much in every way" (3:2) affirms the special status of Israel without negating his previous argument. The Jews were the ones entrusted with the very words of God (the law). They had the righteous standard of God written by the very hand of God on stone tablets and handed to them personally! They did not need to wonder what God's expectation was, or guess about His standard for righteousness, because they had it in their hands.

Ray Stedman, in his commentary on Romans, tells a great story to illustrate this truth. Imagine a group of people are on a dark island.

A terrible storm is coming that threatens to destroy the island and kill all of the inhabitants. There is a very narrow bridge that connects the island to the safety of the mainland, but the clouds have darkened the moon and stars, and it is pitch black. Suppose each person on the island was given a small penlight to help them find the narrow bridge to salvation (conscience), but a select group of people were given a high beam searchlight (the law). Both groups would still be required to cross the bridge in order to get to safety, but the ones with the searchlight certainly had the advantage. Paul still held to the truth that obedience to the law is what mattered (2:13) but the Jews' advantage was in having the exact standard that must be obeyed.

Objection #2: But He promised!

I know there have been times that I have promised my children something and then, because of their bad behavior, chosen not to follow through with my promise. Judicially and relationally, this seems unfair, and often provoked objections like, "But you promised!" The Jews were struggling with being included in the wrath of God with the Gentiles because God made certain promises to them. If what Paul said was true, didn't that mean God was not keeping His promises and so was actually being unfaithful? The answer— "not at all" was the strongest negative response Paul could find in the Greek language. God's faithfulness is NEVER in question. He cannot be UNFAITHFUL because that would violate His very nature.

To illustrate the depth of God's faithfulness, Paul quoted King David from Psalm 51:4. David had just been confronted with the sins of adultery and murder (Bathsheba and Uriah). He sat under the judgment (wrath) of God, but David was still acknowledging that God was true and faithful. God would fulfill all of His promises to Israel that came through Abraham (great nation, possession of the land, bless those who bless, curse those who curse, etc.,) because the Abrahamic covenant was unconditional. The promises of special relationship with God under the Mosaic covenant (the law) were conditional upon obedience. God's judgment of Israel's disobedience to the law was a proof of His faithfulness; it did not negate it! Again, the Jewish people had a tendency to forget about the importance of obedience.

Objection #3: Doesn't our evil make God look good?

As Paul continued, He took the objections from the credible to the incredible. I imagine that upon hearing the first two objections, the Jewish readers were saying, "yeah... what about that?" Having skillfully answered those objections, Paul then took them further down the road than they would want to go to prove his point. He brought up the logical objection that would follow the other two, but it was an objection the Jewish readers would probably not have voiced. If we are all put under the impossible standard of the law, and we all disobey, doesn't that really make God look even more righteous and so bring glory to Him? So if our sin is actually making God look good, how can He condemn us? In fact, if He does condemn us, He is being unjust (3:5). Paul's answer again was fairly emphatic (certainly not!). That argument would make all judgment from God unjust. In fact, Paul went on to say, if they followed that argument to its logical end, you would be saying that the more evil we do, the more good (glory of God) is revealed (3:8). That line is so foolish Paul concludes that anyone who could believe such a thing deserves whatever condemnation they get! None of his readers would have disagreed with that statement.

Having answered the three objections and pretty much stopped the naysayers, Paul then took his readers further down the path. Now you may be reading this and shaking your head at the audacity of the Jews. Let's not be too quick to judge. There is often an attitude in the church that communicates that God gives special grace to those who are church members, baptized, in leadership, etc. Paul reminded us at this point of the truth that apart from Christ, we are all in same condition - condemned. Americans who worship money and materialism are in the same condition as the Hindu with a shelf of gods. Objections overruled!

Questions to Ponder:

1. Which group of people were most likely objecting to Paul's
   argument?

2. Put the 3 objections in your own words.

3. Have you ever felt that God was unfair? How do you resolve
   those feelings?

4. Does God keep His promises? What promises of God are
   you counting on?

Day 8

♦♦♦♦♦♦♦♦♦♦♦♦♦♦♦♦♦♦♦♦♦♦♦

Pulling Out the Little Book
(Romans 3:9-20)

9 What shall we conclude then? Do we have any advantage? Not at all! For we have already made the charge that Jews and Gentiles alike are all under the power of sin. 10 As it is written: "There is no one righteous, not even one; 11 there is no one who understands; there is no one who seeks God. 12 All have turned away, they have together become worthless; there is no one who does good, not even one." 13 "Their throats are open graves; their tongues practice deceit." "The poison of vipers is on their lips." 14 "Their mouths are full of cursing and bitterness." 15 "Their feet are swift to shed blood; 16 ruin and misery mark their ways, 17 and the way of peace they do not know." 18 "There is no fear of God before their eyes." 19 Now we know that whatever the law says, it says to those who are under the law, so that every mouth may be silenced and the whole world held accountable to God. 20 Therefore no one will be declared righteous in God's sight by the works of the law; rather, through the law we become conscious of our sin.

I'm sure if you have been on an actual hike with a trained trail guide, you have experienced that moment when the guide stops talking and reaches into his pocket to pull out a little book. This book represents years of research and expert documentation for this particular trail. The guide reads a passage from the book and maybe even shows you some pictures to confirm that what he has been sharing along the path is, in fact, the truth.

As we entered this hike through Romans with Paul our trail guide, he began with the fact that the wrath of God was being revealed against all godlessness (1:18). Along the way, he has shown us the downward slide into sin and degradation (1:19-32), the righteous judgment of God upon all (2:1-16), and a special section showing that the Jewish people were also subject to God's righteous judgment (2:17-29). He just finished answering some passionate objections by the Jews (3:1-8), and then he got out his little book to add some expert proof to his teaching. Of course, since the objections were coming from the Jews, the little book was the Old Testament that contained the law of God to which he had been referring.

---

*Underline the phrase **we have already made the charge** in 3:9. Write beside this phrase the references **1:18, 2:9 and 2:12**.*

Conclusion

From the three objections raised in 3:1-8, Paul drew a poignant conclusion which he proclaimed by way of a question. He asked, "After all you have heard, after refuting each objection do you really think we (Jews) are any better (than Gentiles) when it comes to God's righteous judgment?" He posed the question, paused for effect, and then answered emphatically, "Not at all!" (3:9). His conclusion then is the truth that he had already made (1:18; 2:9, 12): Jews and Gentiles were all under sin. As soon as he stated those words and heard the collective gasps from the readers, he quickly got out his little book.

---

*Highlight 3:10-12 with one color, 3:13-14 with another and 3:15-17 with a third. Write the word **character** beside the first section, the word **speech** beside the second and the word **actions** beside the third. Draw a box around 3:18.*

Solid Proof

When trying to convince the Jewish people that they were equally deserving of God's judgment, it made sense to follow up the statement with, *It is written...* (3:10). Paul quoted a number of Old Testament passages that affirmed the truth that all are sinners. These passages were from Psalms, Proverbs, and Isaiah and were put together in a logical fashion to point out to the reader that a person's character, speech, and actions all betray their condition as a sinner.

The first paragraph focuses on the character of sinful mankind. The phrase, *There is no one righteous, not even one* is taken from Psalm 53:1 which says *there is no one who does good.* Paul changed the word "good" to the word "righteous" to fit his argument; in comparison to the righteous standard of God (the law), all are unrighteousness. The next two phrases, *there is no one who understands; no one who seeks God* are taken from Psalm 53:2 where God is seen as looking down from heaven for anyone who understands (puts the concept and need for God together in their mind) or seeks (diligently searches for) God. The implied answer in the Psalm is that no one does and Paul worded his quotation with that in mind. The third set of phrases, *all have turned away; they have together become worthless; there is no one who does good, not even one*, is a quotation of Psalm 53:3 and mirrors the same sentiment as Isaiah 53:6, *all we like sheep have gone astray....* The character of mankind is unrighteous, not good, contrary to God and worthless apart from God. The universal nature of this condition is found in the repeated use of the words "none" and "all." Re-read Romans 3:10-12 with this explanation in mind. Powerful, isn't it?

The second paragraph focuses on the speech of sinful mankind. Combining several Old Testament passages (Psalm 5:9, 140:3, 10:7), Paul communicated that the speech of man begins deep in the throat where death reigns, is articulated by their tongues under the control of the great deceiver and father of lies (John 8:44), flows forth in slander and sarcasm to contaminate and kill like poison from their lips and is characterized by curses (blaming God) and bitterness (reproaching God). Re-read Romans 3:13-14 with this historical background in mind. Convinced?

The third and final paragraph focuses on the actions of sinful mankind quoting from Isaiah 59:7-8. Their murderous actions (feet swift to shed blood) revealed their disdain for the sanctity of human life. The ruin and misery that characterize human civilization can be traced through the ghettos, slums, prisons, civil wars, pollution, and treachery that mark all of history's great civilizations. In a word, the actions of mankind can be characterized by turmoil, the complete absence of peace within and without (3:17). Re-read Romans 3:15-17 after understanding this historical context. It is clear that what Paul was saying was not a new truth!

Paul closes his recitation of truth with a quote from Psalm 36:1, *There is no fear of God before their eyes.* The reason for the rampant sin, degradation, and destruction is traced back to exactly what Paul had said in 1:21, *although they knew God, they neither glorified him as God nor gave thanks to him....* The downward spiral into universal sinfulness began with Adam's decision to act independently of God and has continued through the ages with men who *worshiped and served created things rather than the Creator* (1:25). Unrighteousness, ungodliness, and evil all flow from the heart that has rejected God. Let's pause and think about how our own personal struggles with sinful flesh are related to a choice to act independently of God. Doing what is right in our own eyes, making plans without God, choosing to act contrary to what we know is right are all examples of this kind of independence. Personal relationship with God is a dependent relationship.

---

*Circle **every mouth may be silenced** (3:19), **whole world held accountable** (3:19) and **we become conscious of sin** (3:20).*

The Conclusion Re-stated

Paul's conclusion (that all are alike under sin 3:9) didn't mention the role of the law that was so important to the Jewish people. After bolstering his argument with many Old Testament passages, Paul re-stated his conclusion and put it in terms of the law. The law silenced every objection to God's righteous judgment because no one had kept the whole law. The law revealed the standard by which God judges the world and so holds the entire world accountable for their disobedience. The law also made us conscious of sin. It is God's perfect, holy, pure standard, and anything compared to it looks soiled.

If I were to ask you what color most sheep are, you would say they are white. But let's take a flock of sheep and put them in front of a solid white background, all of the sudden they don't look so white. We may see righteousness as something that is subjective and believe that someone is righteous because they look so much better than someone else. But no matter how much good we do, if we are compared against the backdrop of God's perfect righteousness we will come up short. We all come up short.

Jesus illustrated this last point beautifully in Luke 18. A ruler came to Jesus and asked him, *Good teacher, what can I do to inherit eternal life?* (Luke 18:8). Jesus' first response to the man was that only God is good (righteous). He quoted the law (ten commandments) to the ruler who assured Jesus that he had kept them all. Jesus, of course, knew that was not true so he pointed out the one that was most glaringly being violated. The man had great possessions and was unwilling to give them away (covetousness). Jesus used the law to show this young man his guilt, the ruler saw himself as unrighteous and went away sad because he did not want to let go of his sin.

The conclusion then, stated as simply and emphatically as Paul could muster, is *therefore no one will be declared righteous in his sight by observing the law...* (3:20). Teaching that indicates righteousness is achieved by striving to do good (works), by trying to outweigh bad choices with good choices (penance) or any systematic approach to righteousness (legalism) is NOT the Gospel.

Questions to Ponder:

1. How does Paul amplify his conclusion from verse 9 to verse 20?

2. What glaring evidence do you see in today's world that mankind's character, speech and actions are unrighteous?

3. Why do you think Paul is taking so much time on this subject?

Day 9

♦♦♦♦♦♦♦♦♦♦♦♦♦♦♦♦♦♦♦♦♦♦

Righteousness through Faith
(Romans 3:21-31)

21 But now the righteousness of God apart from law has been made known, to which the Law and the Prophets testify. 22 This righteousness from God comes through faith in Jesus Christ to all who believe. There is no difference, 23 for all have sinned and fall short of the glory of God, 24 and are justified freely by his grace through the redemption that came by Christ Jesus. 25 God presented Christ as a sacrifice of atonement, through faith in his blood. He did this to demonstrate his justice, because in his forbearance he had left the sins committed beforehand unpunished— 26 he did it to demonstrate his justice at the present time, so as to be just and the one who justifies those who have faith in Jesus. 27 Where, then, is boasting? It is excluded. On what principle? On that of observing law? No, but on that of faith. 28 For we maintain that a man is justified by faith apart from the observing the law. 29 Is God the God of Jews only? Is he not the God of Gentiles too? Yes, of Gentiles too, 30 since there is only one God, who will justify the circumcised by faith and the uncircumcised through that same faith. 31 Do we, then, nullify the law by this faith? Not at all! Rather, we uphold the law.

After hiking up a steep path over rocks and roots, swatting bugs out of our faces, breathing hard and sweating, it is always nice to walk out into a clearing and take in a beautiful panoramic view of the surrounding countryside. The difficulty of the trail which we experienced up to this point fades as we take in all of the wonders of God's creation.

In Romans 1:17 the Apostle Paul introduced a very refreshing concept – a Gospel or piece of good news that involved the righteousness of God, given to us by faith. Since the announcement of the Gospel, though, we have been trudging through a discourse on how sinful mankind has become, and the trail has become more and more dark and hopeless (1:18-3:20). As we step out of the darkness of this discussion, Paul introduces a fresh, fuller view of the Gospel with the words, *But now...* (3:21).

*Highlight in the same color the words **through faith** (3:22), **all who believe** (3:22), **by his grace** (3:24), **through faith in his blood** (3:25), **have faith in Jesus** (3:26), **of faith** (3:27), **by faith** (3:28) **by faith** (3:30), **through that same faith** (3:30) **and by this faith** (3:31).*

The Nature of this Righteousness

With those two words "but now," Paul steps out of the darkness of the universal sinfulness of man and the total depravity of the human race and allows us to take in a refreshing view of the Gospel. This Gospel involves a righteousness that is apart from the law. In other words, this righteousness is not received by obeying the law or by doing good deeds. The message of the Old Covenant was that if we could do righteous things (obey the law) we could become righteous. Our identity would be earned by our behavior. The problem is that when we factor in human depravity (all are sinners) the goal becomes impossible. No one can become righteous by doing righteous things. The new covenant, the Gospel, turns it around completely. We do righteous things because we **are** righteous. Behavior flows out of identity, and a whole new identity is given to us by His grace (3:24). It is a free gift that flows from the heart of God, through the blood of Christ, and into our dark hearts. Now we do righteous things because we are righteous.

Imagine that you had a desire to swim underwater for hours without an oxygen tank. In pursuit of that desire you practiced holding your breath underwater and slowly, incrementally increased the amount of time you could swim underwater without an oxygen tank. The problem is that no amount of practice will ever enable you to swim underwater indefinitely without an oxygen tank. You might increase your time, achieve longer times than anyone else you know and even set world records but you will never achieve the goal. You will always fall short... unless God changed you into a fish ☺. This may sound far-fetched but, in a sense, this is exactly what God has done (no not changed you into a fish) but He has changed you into a righteous person, a feat you were never capable of without Him.

Because it is a free gift, it is only available by faith. Since Adam and Eve chose to eat the fruit to get life on their own, apart from God, man has been trying to obtain righteousness by his own actions. This "doing" is so engrained in us that God felt it necessary to repeat the phrase by faith eight times in this passage. In the better part of three chapters now we have heard that we cannot become righteous by doing, but by faith. I imagine the readers were exhausted by the conversation and ready to throw up their hands and say, "Okay, okay, we get it!" But now, in presenting the solution, the same amount of repetition is necessary. This righteousness that can never come through the law is given to us as a gift by faith. We must believe. We must embrace it. We must receive it.

Not only is it only available by faith, but it is available by faith equally to all who believe. Paul has shown that we are all guilty, unrighteous either under the law or apart from the law (condemned by our own conscience). All are sinners (3:23) and all can be declared righteous freely by His grace (3:24). Since all are guilty, all must believe, Jew and Gentile alike.

Circle the words **redemption** *(3:24) and* **sacrifice of atonement** *(3:25).*

The Grounds of this Righteousness

After reading this passage, we could make the assumption that faith or belief is the center of the Gospel. But faith is not the point; faith is the means. It is not our faith itself that makes us righteous; it is the object of that faith, Jesus Christ. We are made righteous by faith **in** Jesus Christ (3:22). The object of the Gospel is a person, the person of Jesus Christ. In John's Gospel, we are told that it is by receiving Him, that we become children of God (John 1:12).

What is it about Jesus that makes us righteous? Two words are used to describe the specific object of our faith. The first is *redemption* (3:24). This word literally means deliverance by paying a ransom. God had told Adam that the price or payment for his sin of disobedience was death (Genesis 2:17). This price must be paid in order to satisfy the righteous demands of God. Christ delivers us from this ransom or debt by his death in our place on the cross. The death of Christ pays the debt in full. It is the cross of Jesus that delivers us, not the teachings of Jesus. Faith in Jesus focuses on faith in His death on the cross for us.

The second word used to describe the object of our faith is translated into English by the phrase *sacrifice of atonement* (3:25). In other places, this Greek word is translated "propitiation." To propitiate means to fully satisfy or appease. This word was used to describe the top of the Ark of the Covenant that was a part of the Old Covenant sacrificial system. This piece of holy furniture was housed in the Holy of Holies section of the Jewish Temple. Only the high priest went into this room and only once a year, on the day of atonement. On that day an animal was sacrificed to atone for or "cover" the sins of the people. The blood of the sacrificial animal was sprinkled on the top of the Ark of the Covenant by the High Priest to satisfy God's demands concerning their sin (death). This sacrifice had to be repeated because the blood of animals could never take away sin (Hebrews 10:4), it could only cover it until the perfect sacrifice could come. Jesus' blood completely satisfies the demand. The justice of God demands that sin be punished and the death of Christ satisfies or propitiates that demand.

God presented Christ as a sacrifice of atonement or a propitiation in order to demonstrate His justice (3:25). As an illustration of this, Paul brought up sins that were committed before Christ died, in other words the sins of the Old Testament. God held back his judgment and allowed that sin to go unpunished for a while, so that in our day, He could demonstrate His justice through the death of Christ and declare all who believe righteous (3:25-26). Remember Paul had started this whole discussion with the truth that the wrath of God was being revealed from Heaven against all ungodliness and unrighteousness (1:18). God poured out His wrath on Jesus, and Jesus endured the death of the cross, including separation from the Father, on our behalf, thus satisfying God's justice. This satisfied God's righteous demands both for the sinners under the Old Covenant and the sinners under the New Covenant.

> *Highlight in the same color the words **righteousness** in 3:21, 22 and **just, justice, justify or justified** in 3:24, 25, 26, 28, 30.*

The Object of this Righteousness

In the introduction to this book, we explored the word *righteous*. The Greek word *dikaiosuna* literally means one who is as he ought to be, one who is right, not simply in what he does but in who he is. In reference to our relationship with God, righteousness is the condition of being accepted by God, completely. Another form of the same Greek word is translated justification throughout Romans. This word means to make someone righteous or to declare them righteous.

This righteousness, apart from law, given as a free gift, is not about what we do, it is about who we are. We are given the gift of righteousness that is an identity. We now become the righteousness of God (II Corinthians 5:21). By faith in Christ's death on the cross, we become a whole new person. Our new identity makes us the person we were always meant to be, and introduces us to the life we were always meant to live, an abundant life (John 10:10). This is what it means to be righteous.

In order to explain the transaction of becoming righteous, Paul used the word "justified." This is actually a judicial term, meaning it is the pronouncement of a verdict. God, the Righteous Judge, declares that we are righteous on the basis of our faith in the death of Christ. Having been declared righteous by God, we are now living in a state of righteousness. We are not becoming righteous through a process of sanctification, we are completely righteous, it is who we are! So while the wrath of God is being revealed from Heaven against unrighteousness (1:18), we have been declared righteous and so will receive no condemnation (8:1).

If this is true, why are we all trying so hard to do better? To pray more? To be more loving? To be more pleasing to God? Most striving is the result of a feeling of inadequacy or unworthiness. Some psychologists say that this drive for value or worth is the prevailing problem of our day. Man has been striving since the Garden of Eden, trying to make life work, trying to be right. Jesus came to offer us rest from striving (Matthew 11:28). When we have been declared right by God, we can rest from striving because life and righteousness will flow out of us. Behavior flows out of identity! We don't pray more, do more or love more in order to be right with God. We do these things because we ARE right with God.

---

*Underline the words **boasting** (3:27), **Jews only** (3:29) and **nullify the law** (3:31).*

The Results of this Righteousness

In his discussion of man's sinfulness, certain thoughts concerning the superiority of the Jews came up. As Paul closed this paragraph, he shared how the Gospel (righteousness by faith) impacts these thoughts.

Paul had answered an objection by the Jewish reader concerning the fact that Jews were God's chosen people and had a special position with God. Jews under the Old Covenant often boasted of their position as children of promise, receivers of the law and heirs of Abraham. One of the clear results of the New Covenant is the elimination of all boasting. We are all unrighteous, deserving of God's wrath, and we all receive God's righteousness completely by faith, not based on any good we have done. Therefore, we have nothing to boast about. Paul repeated this concept to the Christians at Ephesus when he said in Ephesians 2:9 *...not by works so that no one can boast*. Evidently the Jews weren't the only ones who thought they were special.

A companion thought that Paul brought up next flowed naturally from the first. Both Jews and Gentiles receive this righteousness in the same way. God justifies Jew and Gentile by their faith in the finished work of Christ on the cross.

For hundreds of years, the Jewish people had venerated the law and held it up as God's righteous standard. If righteousness does not come through the law, then a logical conclusion might be that the law is no longer in effect and is completely discarded. Paul's answer is another emphatic, "Not at all" (3:31). The law still reflected the righteous standard of God. The law was kept by Jesus as a confirmation of His righteousness and we have received His righteousness. The law remained the same but now, in Christ, we do not fall short!

Questions to Ponder:

1. What is the only way to be made righteous?

2. What are some of the benefits of receiving a whole new identity?

3. Explain HOW we are made righteous?

4. What do righteous people do?

5. How does this truth eliminate striving?

Day 10

◆◆◆◆◆◆◆◆◆◆◆◆◆◆◆◆◆◆◆◆◆◆◆◆

Historical Proof of Righteousness by Faith
(Romans 4:1-17)

1 What then shall we say that Abraham, our forefather, discovered in this matter? 2 If, in fact, Abraham was justified by works, he had something to boast about--but not before God. 3 What does the Scripture say? "Abraham believed God, and it was credited to him as righteousness." 4 Now when a man works, his wages are not credited to him as a gift, but as an obligation. 5 However, to the man who does not work but trusts God who justifies the wicked, his faith is credited as righteousness. 6 David says the same thing when he speaks of the blessedness of the man to whom God credits righteousness apart from works: 7 "Blessed are they whose transgressions are forgiven, whose sins are covered. 8 Blessed is the man whose sin the Lord will never count against him." 9 Is this blessedness only for the circumcised, or also for the uncircumcised? We have been saying that Abraham's faith was credited to him as righteousness. 10 Under what circumstances was it credited? Was it after he was circumcised, or before? It was not after, but before! 11 And he received the sign of circumcision, a seal of the righteousness that he had by faith while he was still uncircumcised. So then, he is the father of all who believe but have not been circumcised, in order that righteousness might be credited to them. 12 And he is also the father of the circumcised who not only are circumcised but who also walk in the footsteps of the faith that our father Abraham had before he was circumcised. 13 It was not through law that Abraham and his offspring received the promise that he would be heir of the world, but through the righteousness that comes by faith. 14 For if those who live by law are heirs, faith has no value and the promise is worthless, 15 because law brings wrath. And where there is no law there is no transgression.

While we stand at the top of this trail and enjoy the beautiful view of God's righteousness, our guide carefully brings up four relevant arguments to convince us that what we are taking in, this righteousness of God, really is free when we believe. Since he has been focused on the Jewish reader, he chooses to use Abraham and David, two of the most prominent characters in Jewish history as his examples. Then, he uses the illustrations of circumcision and the Abrahamic covenant to expand the discussion to make it applicable to all nations.

---

*Put number 1 beside **Abraham believed God** (4:3). Put number 2 beside **David says the same thing** (4:6). Put number 3 beside **only for the circumcised** (4:9). Put number 4 beside **received the promise** (4:13).*

Four Proofs

Abraham is often called the father of the faithful, and that thought comes from this passage (4:11). In order to fully understand this passage, we must review the history of Abraham. Abram (his name when God first encountered him) was living in Ur of the Chaldees (Mesopotamia) with his father Terah, his wife Sarai, his brothers Haran and Nahor, and his nephew Lot (Genesis 11:27-30). The Lord called Abram to leave Ur and go to Canaan. At the same time, God made a series of promises to Abram that we now call the Abrahamic Covenant. Among these promises was that God would make him into a great nation and that all nations of the earth would be blessed through him (Genesis 12:1-3). Later when Abram was in his 80's living in Canaan, God came to reassure him of the promises even though Abram and Sarai still had no children. It is here that Abram made the choice to believe in or fully embrace God's promises and the scripture says it was credited to him for righteousness (Genesis 15:6). When Abram was 86, his faith in God faltered, and he went along with a plan to produce an heir through his wife's handmaid, Hagar (he acted independently of God which is NOT faith). The child born to Abram and Hagar was named Ishmael, but he was not the child of promise (Genesis 16). When Abram was 99, God again appeared to him to confirm the

Covenant. This time, God instituted the circumcision of all male heirs of Abram as an outward physical sign of the Covenant he made with Abram and changed Abram's name to Abraham. That very year, God visited Sarai (name was changed to Sarah) and she conceived, finally giving birth to the promised son, Isaac (Gen. 21).

Paul's first proof of the truth of righteousness by faith was when he said that Abraham believed God, and it was credited to him for righteousness (4:3). The word for credited here means to "reckon," not as an opinion but as a fact. I reckon I have $30 doesn't mean I might have $30, it means I have $30. Another definition takes the meaning a little farther toward the concept of imputation and communicates that God put righteousness in Abraham's account (so God knows it is there). The point here was not the giving of the righteousness, it was about the motivation for the gift. If God gave it because Abraham worked for it or deserved it based on his own works, he would be allowed to brag about his status, even able to brag to God. Not only that, but since what we earn is actually owed to us as an obligation, God would owe Abraham this righteousness so it would be more of a payment than a gift. The Scriptures both here and in Genesis make it clear that it was Abraham's belief or faith that prompted God to give him the gift of righteousness. Abraham was right with God because Abraham believed, not because he did good works. The father of the Jewish nation was justified (declared righteous by God) because of his faith, not because of his works. His faith required action (he had to move to Canaan). His faith was in the goodness of God and his faith was imperfect. When we place our faith in God's sacrifice of Christ on the cross, it will require action, it will be based on an underlying belief that God is good and it will certainly be imperfect. An imperfect faith in a perfect God is... enough.

The second proof was a reference to King David. One of the unfortunate periods of David's life was when he committed adultery with Bathsheba and had her husband Uriah murdered to cover up the sin. David kept his sin quiet until one day Nathan the prophet showed up and confronted him. David recorded that when he kept his sin quiet and covered up, he was miserable (Psalm 32:3-4), but when he believed the message of Nathan the prophet who said his sin was forgiven, he was blessed or happy. Not only was his sin forgiven but it would never be counted against him. He received forgiveness and was right with God, not because he had done right, but because God graciously gave him the gift of forgiveness. The same word that is used of Abraham is used of David. God credited him righteousness (4:6). This time, Paul adds the phrase "apart from works." He had already taught them that this righteousness was apart from the law (3:21), but then he added that this righteousness was apart from works (4:6). God's deliverance is not one part faith and one part works. It is all faith.

Paul turned back to the story of Abraham for his third proof. There was a strong movement in the early church by Jewish Christians to require circumcision after a person came to faith. Paul asked the readers to discern at what point in Abraham's life he was given this gift of righteousness. Was it when he was circumcised or uncircumcised? Abraham received righteousness in Genesis 15 and was circumcised in Genesis 17 along with his son Ishmael. The righteousness of God, given to Abraham, the father of the Jews, had nothing whatsoever to do with circumcision.

Finally, Paul used the Abrahamic Covenant as proof of righteousness by faith. He promised Abraham that he would be the father of many nations. Paul is telling us that all who, like Abraham, put their faith in God become the children of Abraham. This promise was made before the law of circumcision was instituted. Circumcision, as a part of the law, does not make one a child of Abraham; faith does. If we became children of Abraham by the law, we would all be disqualified as Paul made clear in the previous chapters. If we were heirs of Abraham's promise by law, we would all die.

---

*Underline the phrases that contain both the words **credited** and **righteousness** in 4:3,5,6,11.*

The Credit to our Account

Just like his repetition of the word faith in 3:21-31, Paul repeated the phrase *credited as righteousness* several times in this passage. This is the Gospel. We are all sinners, deserving of the wrath of God, but God sends Jesus to satisfy those righteous demands through His death on the cross. Our faith in that sacrifice triggers God to declare us righteous judicially and put his righteousness in our account. We don't have righteousness, we are righteous and it is not our righteousness, it is His. Picture God sitting at the seat of judgment, gavel in hand. As the gavel lowers, He doesn't just say "not guilty" he also pronounces us "righteous".

I had a friend who had an old car in his garage. The engine was completely dead and he had been told it needed a new engine. It would be foolish of him to put new tires on the car, replace the headlights, upholstery, and windshield wipers in an effort to get the car on the road. The problem went deeper than that. It went to the very core of the car. Our problem is that we are sinners in the core of our being. It is our identity and in this identity we are unacceptable to God. Obedience to the law can help us clean up our behavior a little but it has no power to give us a new identity. Faith in the cross of Jesus apart from the law and apart from any good works on our behalf triggers the power of the gospel to remove sin, declare us righteous and gives us a new identity, making us acceptable to God.

Questions to Ponder:

1. What impresses you the most about Abraham's faith? How is it like saving faith?

2. Put the 4 proofs Paul offers here in your own words.

3. Imagine yourself in the courtroom as the gavel comes down, how do you respond to God's pronouncement?

Day 11

◆◆◆◆◆◆◆◆◆◆◆◆◆◆◆◆◆◆◆◆◆◆◆◆◆

Understanding Faith
(Romans 4:16-25)

16 Therefore, the promise comes by faith, so that it may be by grace and may be guaranteed to all Abraham's offspring--not only to those who are of the law but also to those who are of the faith of Abraham. He is the father of us all. 17 As it is written: "I have made you a father of many nations." He is our father in the sight of God, in whom he believed--the God who gives life to the dead and calls things that are not as though they were. 18 Against all hope, Abraham in hope believed and so became the father of many nations, just as it had been said to him, "So shall your offspring be." 19 Without weakening in his faith, he faced the fact that his body was as good as dead--since he was about a hundred years old--and that Sarah's womb was also dead. 20 Yet he did not waver through unbelief regarding the promise of God, but was strengthened in his faith and gave glory to God, 21 being fully persuaded that God had power to do what he had promised. 22 This is why "it was credited to him as righteousness." 23 The words "it was credited to him" were written not for him alone, 24 but also for us, to whom God will credit righteousness--for us who believe in him who raised Jesus our Lord from the dead. 25 He was delivered over to death for our sins and was raised to life for our justification.

I remember once being on a hike with a man who was constantly bringing up how important it was to have the right shoes for hiking. When climbing up a steep hill, he would say, "Proper hiking shoes should provide good traction." When going through a small stream he would say, "The right hiking shoes should be waterproof." When hiking over rough terrain, he would say, "The correct hiking shoes are sturdy enough to withstand this trail." Near the end of the hike he said, "The right hiking shoes should still be comfortable after this long hike." Finally someone asked the question that he had hoped they would ask, "What are the right hiking shoes?" That's when he revealed he was a distributor for Red Wing Shoes that had a new line of hiking boots.

We've been hiking awhile through Romans with Paul. We have heard him say that the Gospel is the power of God to everyone who believes or has faith (1:16). He has said that the righteousness of God comes by faith (3:21), that God justifies by faith (3:28), and righteousness is credited to us by faith (4:5). It's about time we asked the question, "What is faith?" To this Paul answers, "I'm glad you asked."

---

*Underline **the promise comes by faith (4:16)**, **that it may be by grace (4:16)** and **may be guaranteed (4:16)**.*

The Promise Comes by Faith

Paul justifies his repetition of the concept of faith by stating that it is by faith that the promise comes to us. The promise of righteousness is not available by law or by works but only by faith. Remember that righteousness is rightness or being what one was always meant to be. When we are declared righteous, we are accepted by God and we receive value and worth. Lack of acceptance, value, and worth drive many addictions, dysfunctional relationships, and greed. This lack creates a void in us. Whenever we feel the void we attach to something that seems to fill the void temporarily (food, TV, sex, pornography, alcohol, drugs, shopping, etc.,). The attachment doesn't completely fill the void so we become obsessed with trying to make it work, creating a greater feeling of unacceptance and worthlessness. No amount of striving will reverse this downward spiral. The answer is the gift of righteousness that is only available by faith.

The fact that this promise is only available by faith, not works or law, means that the promise cannot be earned in any way by our own behavior. It comes by grace. It is a gift, an undeserved gift. Receiving a free gift always makes the recipient feel special.

Taking the law out of the equation opens up the gift to those who were never placed under the law (Gentiles).

The fact that the promise comes by grace guarantees the promise itself because it is given as a free gift and is not dependent on us at all. We cannot do anything to mess up this gift of righteousness, because it has nothing to do with us. It is His righteousness given to us by faith, so it is a guarantee. When people doubt their salvation or standing with God, it is usually because of something they did wrong or the absence of something they should have done right. Works. Since our righteousness does not depend on our behavior, but only comes by grace through faith – nothing can change it; it is guaranteed. Most of the time when a Christian sins, feels bad and begins to think "I must not be saved", the question itself is proof of the indwelling work of the Holy Spirit. Sin in the life of a Christian cannot "undo" what Christ has done.

> *Put a box around the word* **God** *(4:17). Put a number 1 beside* **the God who gives life** *and a number 2 beside* **and calls things that are not as though they were.**

The Object of our Faith

The faith that brings the promise is a faith in God. The quantity or quality of our faith is not nearly as important as the object of our faith. If we trust in something that is not trustworthy, it doesn't matter how much we trust in it because it is incapable of delivering what we need. Jesus said we only need a little faith to move a mountain, as long as that faith is in the God who created the mountain. Paul uses two phrases to describe this God who is the object of our faith. Of course, he could have made a huge list of God's attributes and works, but he only mentions two.

First, He is the God Who gives life. God is the source of all life. In the Garden of Eden life flowed from God into Adam; it was Adam's connection to God that gave him life. When he lost that connection, he died. Jesus comes as the perfect sacrifice for the sin that disconnected us from the source of life. He removes the sin and reconnects us to the source of life, the Father. He told His disciples that He was *the way, the truth and the life; no one comes to the Father but through me* (John 14:6). Jesus also said that his whole purpose in coming was to give life, abundant life (John 10:10). Jesus didn't just die so that we could go to heaven one day. Jesus died to give us life. This God in whom we put our trust is a God of life. He brings the dead back to life every time someone puts their faith in Him. Life is only found in Him.

Second, He is the God who calls things that are not as though they were. This is a reference to God's role as Creator. Paul has already used creation as a proof of the existence of God (1:20) and now points to God's power to create as a part of His definition.

These may seem like random definitions for God, but Paul uses them because of the story he is telling, the story of Abraham. Abraham's faith was in the promise of a son. However Abraham's body was sexually dead (4:19). He could not produce life because he had no sperm. But Abraham trusted in the God Who could bring dead things to life. Sarah's womb was also dead. In other words, she was not producing any eggs. No problem; Abraham trusts in the God Who can call things that are not as though they were! When the time was right, Abraham's sexuality came to life and eggs appeared in Sarah. The object of their faith was very important. No amount of striving or trying would have produced an offspring for this geriatric couple, it had to be the power of God.

Sometimes we place our faith in something that we believe God is going to do rather than in God Himself. We have a loved one who is gravely ill and we have faith that God will heal them. We lose our job and have faith that God will provide us with a new job in a certain amount of time. We struggle in a relationship and we have faith that God will bring harmony. Having faith in God is different than having faith in something we think God will do. God doesn't always do things the way we think He will. We simply trust Him, because of who He is and because of His great love for us, knowing He is well able to do more than we could ever ask.

---
*Circle the words **against all hope** (4:18) and **unbelief regarding the promise of God** (4:20). Underline **strengthened in his faith** (4:20) and **being fully persuaded** (4:21).*

Obstacles to Faith

So, do you want the gift of righteousness? Just believe! It sounds easy doesn't it? But faith is not always easy. Abraham was faced with impossible circumstances. From a human perspective, it looked hopeless. There was no sperm and no egg, but there was supposed to be a conception. Abraham chose to believe God in spite of the impossible. We also find ourselves up against impossible circumstances, but we can choose to believe in the God of the impossible!

Abraham also had to overcome the enormity of the promise God was making to him. He was just a local boy, a herder, nothing special. God appeared one day and told him he will become a great nation and that all nations will be blessed through him. This was too good to be true. How could he let himself believe this? If he did, would he end up being disappointed? But Abraham did not stagger at the promise, in spite of its enormity. He trusted that God was able to do what He promised.

In both cases, Abraham's faith overcame the obstacles, but nothing was said about how much faith he had. Remember that Jesus said it only took a little faith to move a mountain. Abraham's little faith overcame the obstacles and because he believed, his faith grew. The Scripture says it was strengthened to the point that he was fully persuaded that God could fulfill the promise. His faith may have started out shaky; in fact, his scheme with Hagar kind of proves that it was. However, as he continued to move forward in faith, he eventually became fully persuaded. Faith grows to assurance and assurance brings peace.

Questions to Ponder:

1. How does the fact that salvation comes by faith guarantee
   the promise?

2. What would you say to a believer who doubts their
   salvation?

3. Paul used examples of God's power that related to the
   obstacle Abraham faced. Think about an obstacle to
   your faith. What truth about God can help   increase your
   faith?

4. How do we misplace our faith?

Day 12

♦♦♦♦♦♦♦♦♦♦♦♦♦♦♦♦♦♦♦♦♦♦♦♦

Taking in the View
(Romans 5:1-11)

1 Therefore, since we have been justified through faith, we have peace with God through our Lord Jesus Christ, 2 through whom we have gained access by faith into this grace in which we now stand. And we rejoice in the hope of the glory of God. 3 Not only so, but we also rejoice in our sufferings, because we know that suffering produces perseverance; 4 perseverance, character; and character, hope. 5 And hope does not disappoint us, because God has poured out his love into our hearts by the Holy Spirit, whom he has given us. 6 You see, at just the right time, when we were still powerless, Christ died for the ungodly. 7 Very rarely will anyone die for a righteous man, though for a good man someone might possibly dare to die. 8 But God demonstrates his own love for us in this: While we were still sinners, Christ died for us. 9 Since we have now been justified by his blood, how much more shall we be saved from God's wrath through him! 10 For if, when we were God's enemies, we were reconciled to him through the death of his Son, how much more, having been reconciled, shall we be saved through his life! 11 Not only is this so, but we also rejoice in God through our Lord Jesus Christ, through whom we have now received reconciliation.

In the northern part of the state of West Virginia, lies Coopers Rock State Forest, with over 12,000 acres of forest. Most people who visit this park find their way to the Coopers Rock scenic overlook. Built in the late 1930's by the Civilian Conservation Corps, Cooper's Rock provides a breathtaking view. Hundreds of feet below, the Cheat River flows swiftly, a favorite for white water rafting enthusiasts. You can see rock-faced cliffs, layers and layers of mountains that fade into blue in the distance and, on a clear day, you can see all of the way to the city of Morgantown nearly six miles away.

> *Highlight the phrase* **since we have been justified through faith**
> *(5:1). Now circle the word* **peace** *(5:1),* **access** *(5:2),* **rejoice in**
> **our sufferings** *(5:3),* **hope** *(5:4), and* **love** *(5:5). Draw a line from*
> *the phrase you highlighted to each of these words.*

The Gospel Overlook

On our hike through the book of Romans, we find ourselves standing at another overlook, the view equally as breathtaking. It is the view of the Gospel, the good news that we have been justified by faith. Paul has led us up the painful path that convinced us that we were all ungodly, that the law and works could not make us righteous, and that the wrath of God was waiting to be revealed to us. Then the steep trail seemed to level out as he shared this concept of justification by faith. Using the example of Abraham, who before the law, before circumcision, and before the development of organized religion, was declared righteous because of his faith, Paul gave us the good news: we are justified, declared righteous, approved, and accepted by God simply by believing in the finished work of Christ.

That brings us to this overlook. Paul pauses here to help us take in all that this righteousness by faith includes. He quickly points out five things, each a part of this Gospel: peace, access, joy, hope, and love. While we catch our breath, he shares a little about each one.

Because of the sacrificial death of Christ on our behalf, we have been made acceptable to God and we now find ourselves completely at *peace* with Him. Peace simply means that the war is over! We may not have been aware that we were in a war, but we actually were the enemies of God (James 4:4). Sin was in us, flesh was controlling us, Satan was influencing us, and we were moving away from God, ready for His wrath to be poured out on us. But now, the war is over; we are at peace with God. We are no longer sinners in the hands of an angry God. We are saints in the arms of a loving God. We are at peace because our fear of God's wrath, our fear of death, and our fear of Satan has been removed by His acceptance. As we fully embrace this peace, all frantic striving ceases. This peace is not necessarily a feeling, it is a present reality. Through Christ we have peace with God, period! Often we tend to confuse the fact of our peace with a feeling. We feel the tension of living in a sinful world and in a body that has developed sinful flesh patterns. The FACT of our peace can help change the FEELING.

In our new position of acceptance by God, we are granted *access* into His presence (it is easy to approach someone with whom you are at peace). The word access means "approach" or the "ability to move into." We can approach God (Hebrews 10:19,22). As we approach Him, everything that is in His presence is now accessible to us. This includes His grace. He doesn't just give enough grace to save us from wrath, He gives enough grace for us to stand in. We are surrounded by it. God's grace is in front of me, behind me, beside me, over me, and under me. We are immersed in God's grace. It covers all of our sin, past, present, and future. The acceptability, worth, and righteousness we receive from God at salvation is constant and secure because we are standing in God's grace. As we fully embrace the reality of living with a constant awareness of His presence, we can relax, rest.

As Paul introduces *joy* , the third blessing of the gospel, he approaches it from a strange direction. Just as we are beginning to relax, Paul begins to talk about suffering. Suffering doesn't seem to fit in a discussion about peace and grace and certainly not as an introduction to joy. But remember, Jesus told His disciples that He had come to bring peace, but that as long as they were in this world, they could expect trouble (John 16:33). Suffering is a reality of our earthly journey that does not change when we become Christians. What does change is the way we see suffering. Since we are acceptable to God, at peace with God, and immersed in His grace, our suffering can have no long-term effects on us. No matter how much we suffer, 100 years from today, we know that we will be living in His presence. Not only is the outcome secure, the suffering also produces character in us as we persevere. So when we go through trouble, we can actually rejoice, focusing on what the suffering is producing in us and the suffering's lack of real power over us. Rejoicing in suffering is a theme in the Epistles because the early church experienced so much persecution from the world around it (I Peter 4:12, James 1:2, Philippians 1:29, 4:4). As we fully embrace the truth about suffering, our heart rejoices in spite of our circumstances.

Our suffering is overridden by our sense of *hope*. Our confident expectation is that the future includes the glory of God who will be revealed one day, and we will fully participate in it. The glory of God in the Old Testament marked His presence. The glory of God hovered over the Ark of the Covenant and led the children of Israel through the wilderness. The glory of God appeared through Jesus on the Mount of Transfiguration, and the Father spoke a blessing over His Son. Wherever the glory is, God is present. So, our hope is that we will be enveloped one day in the very presence of God, our Creator, our Source. This will be ultimate fulfillment and satisfaction. I recently saw a movie entitled, *The Most Exotic Marigold Hotel*. In the movie a young man in India is trying to refurbish an old hotel and attract retirees from Europe to come there because of the cost of living. Unfortunately the guests begin to arrive before he has the place ready, and they begin to complain. One line that the hotel manager says to the disgruntled residents is, "It will all be okay in the end, so if it is not okay, it is not the end." This is very true for us. It really will all be okay in the end. This is our hope and it leads us forward. Embracing our hope allows us to keep moving forward.

Paul saves the best for last. In 5:5, Paul mentions the *love* of God and the Holy Spirit for the first time in his Epistle to the Romans. The Holy Spirit of God and the love of God have been poured out freely into us. We don't have to ask God to make us loving, we have His love in us through the Person of the Holy Spirit. Often, we think of the Holy Spirit as the One who convicts of sin. This view of Him will probably cause us to fear Him, which will make it really hard for us to surrender to Him or yield our will to Him. It is much easier to yield to the Spirit when we see Him as the source of God's love in us. His main motivation is love. This love is not how God feels about you; it is the very nature of God. God is love and He has given us a new nature which is love. Again don't confuse the fact with the feeling. No matter how you feel at any given moment, the truth is you are loved, you have been filled with love and you are by your new nature a very loving person. This is why we are told that the greatest commandments are to love. God not only gave us this command but He has also given us the capacity to obey the command because we have the love of God in us. As we absorb His love, we are able to show His love to others (I John 4:11). Embracing the love of God in us makes us a loving person.

Now that we have taken in the entire panoramic view of righteousness by faith, let's tie it all together. Faith in the death of Christ makes us acceptable to God and we can settle into a relationship with Him (*peace*). In this relationship, we have *access* to enough grace to allow us to *hope* and *rejoice* through our trials because we know how things end. As we endure, we experience this new life as it was always meant to be by *loving* others with the love that is shed abroad in our hearts.

> *Underline the words **powerless** (5:6), **ungodly** (5:6), **sinners** (5:8) and **enemies** (5:10). Highlight the words **justified** (5:9), **saved** (5:9), **reconciled** (5:10), **saved** (5:10) and **reconciliation** (5:11).*

Perspective

Having introduced the love of God in 5:5, Paul wants to make sure we understand the depth of His love for us. Christ died for us, not when we were good, not when we were trying to obey the law, not when we showed an interest in Him, but when we were powerless, ungodly, sinners and enemies of God. He points out that there are rare examples in the world of people who have been willing to die for a righteous or good man, but it took a depth of love far beyond the reach of mortal man to be willing to die for the ungodly. This is a love that we have never experienced, but it has been forever proven to us by the fact that Christ died coupled with our condition when He chose to do so. We are loved!

Not only were we loved when Christ died, but we are loved now. Paul makes the point that if God loved us enough to let Christ die for us when we were His enemies, how much more will he love us now that we are at peace with God. Paul expands on the word "justified" that he has been using and adds the words "saved" and "reconciled." These are not in addition to our justification; they are nuances of our justification. God has declared us completely righteous. In doing so, He has saved or delivered us from His wrath and He has reconciled us to Him, reconnected us so that a close, intimate relationship is possible.

It might be good to pause at the end of reading this chapter and just stand at the overlook. Take in all that God has given us through Christ. As you do, heave a heavy sigh and relax!

Questions to Ponder:

1. Elaborate on your experience with the five benefits of the gospel shared in this lesson.

2. What is our condition before Christ died for us?

3. What role does hope play in our daily lives?

Day 13

◆◆◆◆◆◆◆◆◆◆◆◆◆◆◆◆◆◆◆◆◆◆◆◆◆

Who Will You Follow?
(Romans 5:12-21)

12 Therefore, just as sin entered the world through one man, and death through sin, and in this way death came to all men, because all sinned-- 13 for before the law was given, sin was in the world. But sin is not taken into account when there is no law. 14 Nevertheless, death reigned from the time of Adam to the time of Moses, even over those who did not sin by breaking a command, as did Adam, who was a pattern of the one to come. 15 But the gift is not like the trespass. For if the many died by the trespass of the one man, how much more did God's grace and the gift that came by the grace of the one man, Jesus Christ, overflow to the many! 16 Again, the gift of God is not like the result of the one man's sin: The judgment followed one sin and brought condemnation, but the gift followed many trespasses and brought justification. 17 For if, by the trespass of the one man, death reigned through that one man, how much more will those who receive God's abundant provision of grace and of the gift of righteousness reign in life through the one man, Jesus Christ. 18 Consequently, just as the result of one trespass was condemnation for all men, so also the result of one act of righteousness was justification that brings life for all men. 19 For just as through the disobedience of the one man the many were made sinners, so also through the obedience of the one man the many will be made righteous. 20 The law was added so that the trespass might increase. But where sin increased, grace increased all the more, 21 so that, just as sin reigned in death, so also grace might reign through righteousness to bring eternal life through Jesus Christ our Lord.

One of my favorite parts of hiking is the scenic overlooks. I can think of many beautiful vistas that I have seen: near a volcano in Indonesia, by a beautiful lake in Albania, at the top of Stony Man on the Blue Ridge Parkway, and from the top of the Eiffel Tower in Paris. However, the most breathtaking view I have experienced was from the top of Corcovado Mountain in Rio de Janeiro, Brazil. Standing beside the 125-foot tall statue of Christ the Redeemer, you can see Sugarloaf Mountain, Copacabana Beach, Guanabara Bay, and the sprawling city of Rio. The view of the city is beautiful and stands in contrast to the view from the bottom of the mountain where *favelas* (Brazilian slums) mar the beauty. It's the same city but a different view.

In a similar way now Paul begins to show us a different view of humanity. He compares and contrasts humanity from Adam's perspective and humanity from Christ's perspective. It is not difficult to see which is preferred.

---

*Highlight the phrase **Adam, who was a pattern** (5:14). Draw a line from **Adam** (5:14) to the words **trespass of the one man** (5:15), **one man's sin** (5:16), **trespass of the one man** (5:17), **disobedience of the one man** (5:19). Circle the words **death reigned** (5:14), **death reigned** (5:17) and **sin reigned in death** (5:21).*

The First Adam

Paul uses the illustration of Adam in contrast to Christ in order to show the scope of our problem and the scope of God's solution. As you just marked from the passage, Adam was guilty of a trespass. God had instituted a law, not a system of laws, but just one law. He was forbidden to eat of the tree of knowledge of good and evil. If he trespassed the law, he would die. Adam's trespass was a sin. It violated the relationship with God because it represented Adam's attempt to find life independent of God. It was also direct disobedience to God's command.

The result of Adam's trespass (disobedience) was that sin and death reigned over the human race. Through this one act Adam had plunged the entire human race into the tyranny of sin and death. This is a summary of what Paul had developed in Romans

1-3. Adam's sin led to the universality of sin and now the universality of death, all of which flowed from Adam's choice to disobey God's command. All have sinned so all must die.

The view of humanity from Adam's perspective is very dismal. All have sinned, so all will experience death. But Adam is not the end of the story.

---

*Highlight the phrase, **of the one to come** (5:14). Draw a line from that phrase to the phrases **grace of the one man, Jesus Christ (5:15), gift of God (5:16), the gift (5:16), God's abundant provision of grace (5:17), gift of righteousness (5:17), one act of obedience (5:18)** and **obedience of the one man (5:19)**. Circle the words **reign in life (5:17)** and **grace might reign through righteousness to bring eternal life (5:21)**.*

The Second Adam

In Corinthians, Paul calls Jesus *the last Adam* (I Corinthians 15:45). In Romans, Paul compares Adam to Christ and says that Adam is a pattern or picture of the *one to come* (5:14). Like Adam, Jesus accomplished something by one act. But His was an act of obedience, not of disobedience. He had come to do the Father's will, and he accomplished what the Father had sent Him to accomplish. Jesus was always obedient to the Father; in His actions, in His teaching, and in His attitudes. But it was not this obedience that solved the universal problem of sin and death. It was the one act of obedience, going to the cross, that brought to us the gift of righteousness, God's abundant provision of grace. In contrast to sin and death, Jesus brought righteousness and life. His death broke the law of sin and His resurrection broke the law of death (the Gospel). The obedience that led Him to the cross is contrasted with the disobedience of Adam. While Adam brought sin and death through one trespass, Jesus brought life and righteousness in spite of many trespasses (5:16). The obedience of Jesus completely undoes the disobedience of Adam!

This discussion sets up a paradigm of belief that may help to simplify the way we see ourselves before God. There are only two Adam's mentioned in this paradigm. The first Adam plunged us into sin and thus brought death upon us. The second Adam obeyed God, defeated the law of sin and death and gives us righteousness and eternal life. So which Adam are you in? There are no other possibilities and there are no mixtures of the two. Paul has taught us that by our faith, we are declared righteous and are placed in Christ. If we are in Christ then we are no longer in Adam. Therefore to define ourselves as "sinners" after we have received Christ's righteousness is incorrect. We are children of God, sanctified, cleansed, forgiven, accepted, beloved and destined for eternity with God. My behavior does not have the power to place me back in Adam.

The Effect of the Law

In the middle of this comparison between Adam and Jesus, Paul gives us a little more insight into the role of the law. Adam had a law put on him that he disobeyed and that disobedience brought death. But humanity was not put under that same law so they *did not sin by breaking a command (5:14)* like Adam. In spite of the fact that between the time of Adam and Moses, there was no law, *sin was in the world* (5:13) and *death reigned* (5:14). There was still sin apart from the law, but that sin was not taken into account because there was no law (5:13).

So why did death reign? If there was no trespass of the law, there could be no condemnation. All of humanity was in Adam when he disobeyed in the garden. We, including those who lived between Adam and Moses, are guilty of the act of the one man, Adam. So, everyone who is born from Adam is born a sinner because they sinned in Adam. This is called original sin and is usually referred to in the *Bible* as the word "sin" (singular) while the word "sins" (plural) refers to our individual disobedience. Sin (original sin) entered the world through one man (5:12) and that sin (original sin) reigned in death (5:21). We could enter into a very complicated theological discussion here about how we were present in Adam when he sinned (federal headship, seminal headship, etc.,) but the bottom line is that Paul is teaching us that we were IN Adam when he sinned and that his sinful nature was passed down to subsequent generations.

So, even apart from the law, we are all guilty before God. The entrance of the law actually increased the amount of trespass. God communicated His righteous standard through the law, and humanity immediately began to trespass that standard, adding sin upon sin (sins). The law increased sin (5:20) which means it is ridiculous to try to overcome sin by the law.

Who is Justified?

Some confusion has arisen out of Paul's use of the word "all" in 5:18. The doctrine of universalism teaches that all men are saved by the death of Christ, whether they believe or not. This teaching is supported by Paul's use of the word all. However, we need to keep 5:18 in context. The preceding verse (5:17) states that *...those who receive God's abundant provision of grace...* are justified and the following verse (5:19) says that *many* (not all) will be made righteous. Clearly Paul is not teaching universal salvation.

Super-abundant Grace

Paul began this chapter rejoicing in the fact that we are totally immersed in God's grace; in fact, we are standing in it (5:2). Now, as he develops the doctrine of righteousness by faith, he talks about God's abundant provision of grace (5:17) and grace increasing (5:20) and reigning (5:21). Grace is God's operating system. It is the only way that He can be in relationship with humanity because He is holy. His grace extended to us through the death of Christ is so abundant that it actually overpowers universal sin and death and reigns over us, bringing us righteousness and eternal life (5:21).

Questions to Ponder:
1. Contrast what we received in the 1st Adam with what we received in the 2nd Adam.

2. How does this chapter highlight how impossible it is to be declared righteous by the law? How does it reinforce our security in Christ?

Day 14

♦♦♦♦♦♦♦♦♦♦♦♦♦♦♦♦♦♦♦♦♦♦♦

Dead or Alive?
(Romans 6:1-14)

1 What shall we say, then? Shall we go on sinning so that grace may increase? 2 By no means! We died to sin; how can we live in it any longer? 3 Or don't you know that all of us who were baptized into Christ Jesus were baptized into his death? 4 We were therefore buried with him through baptism into death in order that, just as Christ was raised from the dead through the glory of the Father, we too may live a new life. 5 If we have been united with him like this in his death, we will certainly also be united with him in his resurrection. 6 For we know that our old self was crucified with him so that the body of sin might be done away with, that we should no longer be slaves to sin-- 7 because anyone who has died has been freed from sin. 8 Now if we died with Christ, we believe that we will also live with him. 9 For we know that since Christ was raised from the dead, he cannot die again; death no longer has mastery over him. 10 The death he died, he died to sin once for all; but the life he lives, he lives to God. 11 In the same way, count yourselves dead to sin but alive to God in Christ Jesus. 12 Therefore do not let sin reign in your mortal body so that you obey its evil desires. 13 Do not offer the parts of your body to sin, as instruments of wickedness, but rather offer yourselves to God, as those who have been brought from death to life; and offer the parts of your body to him as instruments of righteousness. 14 For sin shall not be your master, because you are not under law, but under grace.

Snakes are a part of God's creation that I just don't like. The way they slither along the ground is creepy, and the quickness with which they strike is scary. In my mind, the only good snake is a dead snake, especially if you see one along the hiking trail. Imagine if you will that on your hike through the woods, your guide stops everyone abruptly and points to an object in the middle of the trail ahead. Immediately you all identify the object as a snake. Heart rates elevate, breathing quickens, and some begin to step backwards. The guide moves slowly forward with a large stick. The snake doesn't move. Finally he uses the stick to move the snake off to the side, the snake does not respond. The guide is able to discern that the snake is indeed dead (my favorite kind!). It really does make a difference whether the snake is dead or alive.

> *Put a box around the phrase **we died to sin** (6:2). Underline the phrases **baptized into his death** (6:3), **buried with him** (6:4), **united with him like this in his death** (6:5), **old self was crucified** (6:6), **if we died with Christ** (6:8) **and count yourselves dead to sin** (6:11). Draw a line from the box to each underlined phrase.*

Should we just keep on sinning?

Paul spent the last half of chapter 5 convincing us that our problem does not stem from our behavior (disobedience to the law) but from our birth (we were born in Adam). Therefore, when we experience a new birth and move from being in Adam to being in Christ, our problem is solved. We were sinners in Adam, we are righteous in Christ. This puts the question of the law into perspective. The purpose of the law was not to make us righteous but to magnify the depravity of our condition in Adam and the greatness of God's grace in Christ (5:20).

If you have been closely following Paul's argument up to this point, you probably have the same question in your mind that Paul anticipated and verbalized in 6:1. The law was given to point out our sin, our sin magnifies the grace of God so, should we just keep on sinning so that there will be even more grace? Paul used a continuous present tense verb that literally means to settle down into and then added the noun for sin. The question literally is, "Should we just settle down into a lifestyle of sin, so that there will be even more grace?" Even though it is a logical question, the foolishness of it becomes apparent as we verbalize it. If the grace of God that gives us the new birth in Christ makes us righteous, how could that lead to a life of sinning? Paul's emphatic answer is a repetition of a phrase he has used before, "By no means!" His answer to the question is actually the theme of the first half of Romans 6. The simple answer is "we died to sin" (6:2).

What does it mean that we died to sin? It doesn't mean that sin is dead in me. In fact, later, Paul talked about the power of sin in our flesh (7:17). It doesn't mean that we have to die to sin or crucify our own flesh. Paul was not asking us to do anything about our condition, he was stating something that has already been done. It doesn't mean that we are in the process of dying to sin (progressive sanctification). Paul used the Greek verb tense (Aorist) that indicates an action that was completed in the past. We died (past tense) to sin. Death is final, we don't have to fear the power of something that is dead. Remember the snake? As soon as we realized it was dead, our cause for fear was completely removed.

In later epistles, Paul does instruct believers to mortify (put to death) the deeds of the flesh (8:13, Colossians 3:5). This is not saying that we have to put the old sinful nature to death over and over again. It is already dead. These verses are referencing individual behaviors of our flesh that were developed when we lived in sin and that continue to reside in us as a pattern. Early in my life I learned to use sarcasm to protect myself from the ridicule and hurt of others. I had a quick wit and could usually come back with something quickly that would disarm the other person. That was a part of my sinful nature. My sinful nature died with Christ on the cross but that pattern of my flesh still resides in me and I must make a choice to put it to death (wholly surrender it) in order to experience the life that Christ came to give me. That flesh pattern has no real power over me unless I choose to give it the power. I would not say I am a sarcastic person (it is not my identity) but I would say that I have developed a flesh pattern of sarcasm that needs to be surrendered. Can you identify some flesh patterns that still reside in you? If not, ask someone that lives with you ☺.

---

*Circle the phrases **baptized into Jesus Christ** (6:3), **united with
him** (6:5), **with him** (6:6), **with Christ** (6:8) and **alive to God in
Christ Jesus** (6:11).*

We Died with Christ

In Romans 5, we learned that when Adam sinned in the Garden of
Eden, we were present **in Adam** and so we sinned with him. His
sin was imputed to us. Now, in Romans 6 we learn that we
participated in Christ's death in the same way because we were **in
Christ**. Our faith places us into Christ (baptized means placed
into). We were not just placed into Jesus Christ, we were also
placed into His death (6:3) and buried with Him (6:4). We were
united with him (6:5) in His death in order that the old self, the
sinner (the one that was in Adam) could be destroyed. Remember
in Adam we are all sinners, but Christ "became sin for us" (II
Corinthians 5:21) and died to cancel out the power and penalty of
sin. In so doing, he cancelled sin's power or mastery over us (6:7).

Okay, that last paragraph was powerful. Did you skim it? Read it
again. We can illustrate this truth by taking two envelopes, one
smaller than the other. Write your name on the smaller envelope
and Christ on the larger. Place your envelope in Christ's. You are
in Christ. Now take the envelope within an envelope and place it
under a stack of books. Allow this to represent the death and
burial of Christ. The books symbolize the judgment of God
against sin that was taken out on Christ (and those who are in
Christ). Now remove the envelope from beneath the books. Christ
rose again to experience life and we rose with Him. We are in
Christ so we have experienced death and resurrection with Him.

The horrible death of Christ on the cross was God pouring out His
wrath (1:18) against ungodliness and unrighteousness. When by
our faith we were placed *in Christ*, that wrath was poured out on
our ungodliness and unrighteousness, and we were born again into
a new family. We are in Christ. Since our problem never
stemmed from our behavior but from our birth, the problem is
solved in Christ because we are born again (John 3:3). How can

God allow a murderer into heaven? How can God allow a rapist into heaven? All of sin deserves God's wrath. In Christ that wrath was poured out at the cross and it is all paid for, in full and no longer define us. There will be NO murderers or rapists in heaven, only former sinners made righteous by the death of Christ.

---

*Highlight the phrases **live a new life (6:4), united with him in his resurrection (6:5), live with him (6:8)** and **alive to God in Christ Jesus** (6:11).*

Being in Christ is not just about His death. Those who are in Christ have also participated in His resurrection. Our old man (in Adam) died with Christ on the cross and our new man (righteous) was raised to live a whole new life, a life where sin does not rule us. Since we died to sin, our lives can no longer be characterized by sin, but our lives will be characterized by God who lives in us. Once this begins to dawn on us, the initial question becomes completely foolish. It is impossible for the spirit of man that is dead to sin and alive to God to keep on sinning! We will learn later that it is not our spirit that sins but our flesh. This has been God's plan all along, to make us new, to raise us to a new way of life. In Isaiah 43:19 and Ezekiel 36:26 God reveals through His prophets His desire to give us new hearts and to do a new thing in us. Paul announced to the Corinthians that in Christ we are a whole new creation (II Corinthians 5:17)! We have been born again, not to live the same old life of sin, but to live the life God always intended us to live. Righteous!

---

*Put a box around Romans 6:11 and highlight the words **count yourself**. Then highlight the words do not let sin reign (6:12), do not offer (6:13) and rather offer (6:13).*

Our Mental Assignment

Having established what it means for a believer to be in Christ, Paul for the first time in this epistle to Romans instructed us to do something. Up to this point, he has been teaching us what happened to the human race and what has been done for us. Now it is time for us to engage our wills and minds and choose to do something about what we know. Paul has just taught us that in Christ we are dead to sin but alive to God; he is asking us to personally count this to be true. The word count is an imperative, the **first command of the book**, and it literally means to reckon or to calculate. The truth of our death to sin and aliveness to God is powerless unless we calculate it to be true in our own lives. Count on it as truth! Remember the snake? We can continue to be afraid of the snake if we don't count on the truth of its death. This is a mental assignment and will require some renewing of our minds which Paul covers later (12:2).

While telling yourself that you are dead to sin but alive to God is important, it must be followed by actions that flow from that belief. If we believe that we are dead to sin, we will engage our will and choose not to allow sin to control our flesh (mortal body). Sin cannot control our spirit which is righteous, but we must choose to let our behavior flow out of that spirit instead of allowing it to flow out of our flesh where sin still dwells (Galatians 5:16). Practically speaking, this will involve the various parts of our body that we use to either follow righteousness or follow unrighteousness. What we see (our eyes), what we hear (our ears), what we say (our mouths), where we go (our feet), what we do (our hands), what we think (our minds), and how we satisfy our sexual desires (our genitals) can either be offered (put at the disposal of) our flesh to be used for unrighteousness or our spirit to be used for righteousness. Because we are righteous in the core of our being, behavior that reflects righteousness is revealing who we really are and behavior that reflects sin is against our true identity and will make us miserable. All of the commands of the New Covenant are given with this in mind. We are not commanded to be kind, forgiving, pray without ceasing, etc., in order to be acceptable to God. We are commanded to do these things (or not do them) so that we can experience living out of our true identity as righteous and live the life we were always meant to live. Righteous!

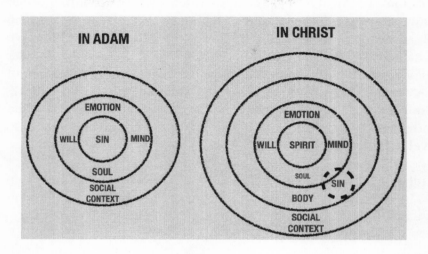

Consider the following chart:

When we were in Adam sin was at the core of who we were. Sin resided in our body, influenced our mind, emotion and will and was lived out in society. Ephesians 2 tells us that in Adam our Spirit was dead so there was no real spiritual dimension to our lives.

But we are no longer in Adam, we are now in Christ. Christ took the sin which was at the core of our being and destroyed it on the cross. He placed His Spirit at the core of our being, giving us a whole new identity which we did not earn (grace). In this way we are completely dead to the tyranny of sin that ruled us in Adam. The Spirit is now free to influence our mind, emotion and will so that we can live out righteousness in society. However, the sinful patterns that we developed when we were in Adam still reside in our flesh (our body). While the Spirit directs us to live as righteous, sometimes our flesh hijacks the righteous deeds and pollutes the righteousness with sin. If you drew a straight line from the Spirit out through the social context on the chart, that would represent what it looks like to live as righteous. If we draw the arrow straight until it gets to our flesh and then turn the line in another direction so that it flows into the social context in a different way than it began, that represents living according ot our flesh. Regardless of our behaviors though, sin is NOT at the core of our being anymore. This sin no longer rules or defines us. We can choose to declare that we are DEAD to this sin and surrender our body to the Spirit of God in us, thus overcoming the deeds of the flesh. Trying to be righteous is living out of the flesh. Allowing righteousness to flow out of our new identity while surrendering the flesh is living life as we were always meant to live! Righteous!

Paul concluded with a reminder in 6:14. Grace has set us free from sin by allowing us to die to sin in Christ. The law could only point out the sinfulness of our sin and so we were kept in bondage. Grace has set us free!

Questions to Ponder:

1. What are all of the things that are true about us because we are in Christ?

2. What is the first real command in the book of Romans? How is this command best obeyed?

3. How does this truth put the commands of the New Testament in perspective?

Day 15

◆◆◆◆◆◆◆◆◆◆◆◆◆◆◆◆◆◆◆◆◆◆◆◆

Whose Slave Are You?
(Romans 6:15-23)

15 What then? Shall we sin because we are not under law but under grace? By no means! 16 Don't you know that when you offer yourselves to someone to obey him as slaves, you are slaves to the one whom you obey--whether you are slaves to sin, which leads to death, or to obedience, which leads to righteousness? 17 But thanks be to God that, though you used to be slaves to sin, you wholeheartedly obeyed the form of teaching to which you were entrusted. 18 You have been set free from sin and have become slaves to righteousness. 19 I put this in human terms because you are weak in your natural selves. Just as you used to offer the parts of your body in slavery to impurity and to ever-increasing wickedness, so now offer them in slavery to righteousness leading to holiness. 20 When you were slaves to sin, you were free from the control of righteousness. 21 What benefit did you reap at that time from the things you are now ashamed of? Those things result in death! 22 But now that you have been set free from sin and have become slaves to God, the benefit you reap leads to holiness, and the result is eternal life. 23 For the wages of sin is death, but the gift of God is eternal life in Christ Jesus our Lord.

Have you ever been hiking on a trail and gotten the feeling that you are going the wrong way? You know that you haven't turned around, and you know that the orange trail markers still indicate you are on the trail, but you just have this feeling. What do you think you should do at this point? Follow the feeling and strike out in the direction you feel is right or continue forward because of what you know? There are probably people still out wandering in the woods because they followed that feeling.

Paul has been teaching a radical truth concerning grace and the law. The law actually increased sin and sin actually makes grace abound. As we have followed this discussion, we have gotten the feeling that this truth actually means it is okay to sin. Paul addressed the feeling in 6:1 and answered it with an emphatic no! It may feel like we are being given permission to live in sin under grace, but that feeling is contrary to the facts, and facts trump feeling! In this passage, Paul has said, *Don't you know?* (6:3), *for we know* (6:6), *for we know* (6:9) and *don't you know* (6:16). He was negating this feeling based on facts!

Highlight the following phrases with the same color: **slaves to sin (6:16)**, **death (6:16)**, **slaves to sin (6:17)**, **slavery to impurity and to ever-increasing wickedness (6:19)**, **slaves to sin (6:20)**, **death (6:21)**, **death (6:23)**.

Slaves to Sin

The fact is that we used to be slaves to sin. As we can clearly see from the words we just highlighted, before Christ we were in bondage to the sin that lived in us because we were in Adam. What is the job description of a slave? It is to do whatever the master says. If sin is our master, sin is the only thing possible for us. He is not saying that we are the slaves to *sins* (our individual acts of wrong). He is referring back to Romans 5 and our condition of being in Adam. When we are living in Adam we are sinners at our core. We are incapable of doing anything that leads to life because we are completely disconnected from the source of life, God. Everything that flows out of that disconnected core is sin. Our sin may have looked good; contributing to the poor, volunteering to feed the homeless, etc., but since it is being done in Adam (independent from God), it is not righteousness, it is sin. No matter how hard we try, our position in Adam keeps us bound to sin and thus, bound to death.

In describing this sin, Paul referred back to his discussion in 1:18-32 and reminded us that slavery to sin involves an ever-increasing wickedness (6:19). Sin grows exponentially, either toward more evil, or toward more human striving to be righteous (which produces only self-righteousness). The good get "gooder" and the bad get "badder." The end result is clear from the passage, death. Death is separation. Those who have not put their faith in Christ will continue to live in Adam separated from the presence of God and will die in Adam living for all eternity separated from God. Sin is a harsh taskmaster, always increasing our burden and leading us to death. The addict requires more of his "medication" to satisfy him as time goes on and he is pulled deeper and deeper into dependency. The religious striver never feels that what he is doing is enough so he keeps saying yes to every opportunity and is well on the way to burnout. The socialite needs to make one more social connection, the businessman needs one more big deal, the athlete needs one more trophy! One may look better than the other but all are sin and we are slaves to it, apart from Christ.

So let's think about how much time we spend trying to be godly. Striving to be more loving, spend more time in prayer, share the gospel more freely are works of our flesh that do not lead to life but lead to bondage and self-righteousness. If we are not disciplined enough to accomplish our goals we feel ashamed and keep trying harder thus becoming slaves to the process. If we are successful in achieving our goals we become self-righteous and look down on others who are not as spiritual as we are. Let's admit that this striving is sin. It doesn't feel like sin but we KNOW it is sin because it is the striving of our flesh.

> *Highlight the following phrases with a different color:* **obedience which leads to righteousness** *(6:16),* **slaves to righteousness** *(6:18),* **slavery to righteousness** *(6:19),* **holiness** *(6:19),* **slaves to God** *(6:22),* **holiness** *(6:22)*, **eternal life** *(6:22) and* **eternal life** *(6:23).*

Slaves to Righteousness

But we are no longer slaves to sin. We know (6:3) that we died to sin in Christ, were buried with Him, and have been raised with Him to a new life of righteousness (6:3-6). Since we died with

Him, we are freed from sin (6:7). Since we are freed from sin, sin can no longer rule over our true self (6:14). We are no longer in Adam so we are no longer sinners at the core of our beings. We have been reconnected to the source of life. We have a new master. We were not simply given power to completely overcome our old master (conquer sin by means of the law), we were given a completely new master. We now serve righteousness. In Christ we have been made righteous. While we were in Adam, sin was at the core of who we were, and the behaviors that flowed from that core were sinful. But now (6:22), in Christ, righteousness is at the core of who we are and the behaviors that flow from that core are righteous. The grace of God not only freed us from the law but also changed us at the core of who we are (II Corinthians 5:17). Sin can no longer flow from our core or true identity because we are righteous. Sin, however, can rule in our flesh (6:12) but when we allow that to happen, we are miserable because we are not living out of our true identity.

So in answer to the question about continuing in sin, Paul told us that grace actually leads to obedience. When we obey, we are living from our righteous core, and that harmonious living is the definition of life. Eternal life is not just Heaven, it is life now, life that flows out in righteousness and reflects the source of life in us. Slavery to sin leads to ever-increasing wickedness (6:19), but slavery to righteousness leads to holiness (6:19, 22). God is holy (Psalm 99:5). It is not an attribute of God, it is His identity. When He lives in us and we live from that core, we live in holiness. So Paul turned the whole discussion around and taught that not only does grace not lead to more sin, it actually leads to holy living! This explains why later Paul talks about a transformation of behavior that actually begins at the core of our being and works its way out (12:1-2).

---

*Circle the phrase **wholeheartedly obeyed the form of teaching to which you were entrusted** (6:17).*

Obedience to the Gospel

When we understand this concept, a new question arises: who wouldn't want to change masters? There are many reading this that have been trying to shake off the slavery to sin by striving to obey the law, do good deeds, serve the Lord, and be a good person. Paul reminds the Romans that if they are no longer the slaves of sin, it is not because they obeyed the law, it is because they obeyed the teaching entrusted to them. The teaching was the Gospel. Paul brought his letter full circle here. He began by telling them He had been set apart for the Gospel (1:1) and that his role was to call people to the obedience that comes from faith (1:5), clearly referring to belief in the Gospel (1:16). In this Gospel, God revealed a righteousness that is by faith (1:17). Obedience to or faith in the Gospel of Christ removes us from our position in Adam and places us in Christ, frees us from slavery to sin, and makes us slaves to His righteousness. Hallelujah!

Questions to Ponder:

1. What does it look like to be a slave to sin?

2. What does it look like to be a slave to righteousness?

3. How do we change masters?

Day 16

♦♦♦♦♦♦♦♦♦♦♦♦♦♦♦♦♦♦♦♦♦♦

Headed in the Right Direction
(Romans 7:1-13)

1 Do you not know, brothers--for I am speaking to men who know the law--that the law has authority over a man only as long as he lives? 2 For example, by law a married woman is bound to her husband as long as he is alive, but if her husband dies, she is released from the law of marriage. 3 So then, if she marries another man while her husband is still alive, she is called an adulteress. But if her husband dies, she is released from that law and is not an adulteress, even though she marries another man. 4 So, my brothers, you also died to the law through the body of Christ, that you might belong to another, to him who was raised from the dead, in order that we might bear fruit to God. 5 For when we were controlled by the flesh, the sinful passions aroused by the law were at work in our bodies, so that we bore fruit for death. 6 But now, by dying to what once bound us, we have been released from the law so that we serve in the new way of the Spirit, and not in the old way of the written code. 7 What shall we say, then? Is the law sin? Certainly not! Indeed I would not have known what sin was except through the law. For I would not have known what coveting really was if the law had not said, "Do not covet." 8 But sin, seizing the opportunity afforded by the commandment, produced in me every kind of covetous desire. For apart from law, sin is dead. 9 Once I was alive apart from law; but when the commandment came, sin sprang to life and I died. 10 I found that the very commandment that was intended to bring life actually brought death. 11 For sin, seizing the opportunity afforded by the commandment, deceived me, and through the commandment put me to death. 12 So then, the law is holy, and the commandment is holy, righteous and good. 13 Did that which is good, then, become death to me? By no means! But in order that sin might be recognized as sin, it produced death in me through what was good, so that through the commandment sin might become utterly sinful.

Peter Potterfield has hiked over 10,000 miles of trails on six continents. In his book, *Classic Hikes of the World*, he shares some of his favorites. Among them is Kungsleden, Sweden, the Kings Trail. Potterfield hiked 65 miles through birch forests, open tundra, beside big glaciers, and then over the shoulder of Sweden's highest peak, Mt. Kebnekaise towering 6,926 feet above sea level. This trail lies 100 miles inside of the Arctic Circle, so it definitely qualifies as a far north trail. On his tips to fellow hikers, Potterfield said that this trail can be hiked in either direction, but he advised traveling from north to south because it keeps the sun on your face, which is no small consideration in the Arctic!

In Romans, Paul wrote to believers about the trail of life. He acknowledged that we can hike this trail in either direction, toward grace or toward law. He strongly recommended that we hike this trail in the direction of grace, because only then does the path lead to life and only then can we daily enjoy the Son before our face.

Paul has been communicating through a series of questions (6:1,14) and he continues using that literary device throughout chapter 7 (7:1,7, 13).

---

*Underline the phrase **you also died to the law** (7:4) and put a number 1 beside it. Underline the phrase **that you might belong to another** (7:4) and put a number 2 beside it. Underline the phrase **in order that we might bear fruit to God** (7:4) and put a number 3 beside it. Highlight the phrase **through the body of Christ** (7:4).*

Don't You Know that Death Releases Us from the Law?

Paul continued his discussion about how grace affects sin. He stated that sin would not be our master because we are not under law but under grace (6:14). We have a new master and have been freed from the tyranny of the law. In chapter 7, Paul uses several illustrations to drive this point home. The first illustration was a simple story of how the law works and is directed at those *who know the law* (7:1). The word "law" can be used in several different ways. Paul most often used it to refer to the law of God, the 613 commandments contained in the Mosaic law, including the Ten Commandments. In 7:1-4, the word is used in a broader sense about the laws of society, particularly those that regulate marriage.

In the illustration a woman was married to a husband. Under law, she was bound to that husband legally in the relationship of husband-wife. If she married another man while her husband was still living, she became an adulteress. However, if that husband died, she was freed from the law of marriage and allowed to marry another without being labeled an adulteress. Death freed her from the law of marriage. The explanation of the illustration is found in verse 4.

First, just like the woman was bound to her first husband by the law, we were bound to sin by the law. The righteous standard of the law held us in a place of condemnation, it bound us. Remember the discussion throughout the last part of chapter 6? We used to be slaves (bound) to sin. But sin died, just like the first husband died. How did sin die? *Through the body of Christ* (7:4)! We were in Christ when He took on the sin of the world and died (6:8) and so we are dead to sin (6:11). Since sin died, we are released from the law just like the wife was released from the law by the death of her first husband. Now we are free to belong to another. We are now married to Christ and instead of being bound to sin, we are bound to righteousness (6:18) not by the law, but by grace.

Consider this chart to illustrate the illustration:

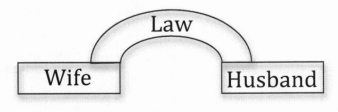

When a woman is married to a man, she is legally bound to him. She is not free to do as she pleases according to the law. But if the husband dies, the law is not

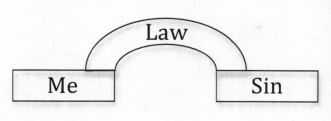

binding her to anything so she is free from the law of marriage. Because we were born with a sinful nature AND born under the law, the law keeps us bound to sin. The commandment is impossible for us to keep so we are bound to sin which leads to death.

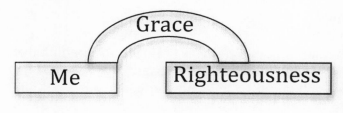

However, Christ's death was also the death of sin (Romans 6). Our sin died with Christ on the cross. Therefore, just like the death of the husband freed the wife from the law of marriage, so the death of sin in Christ frees us from the law. Christ replaced our sin with His righteousness. Now we are bound to His righteousness, not by law, nor by our own behavior but completely by His grace. This is why in Romans 6:13 Paul urges us to yield our bodies to the righteousness to which we are now bound (slaves).

What is the result? We will *bear fruit* (7:4). This fruit is not obedience to the law. In Philippians 1:11, Paul spoke of the fruits of righteousness and in Galatians, he speaks of the Fruit of the Spirit. So once we are freed from the law, what flows out of us? Sin? By no means (6:1, 15)! The grace of God produces love, joy, peace, patience, kindness, goodness, faithfulness, gentleness, and self-control (Galatians 5:22,23).

Having explained the illustration, Paul then emphatically stated his point in 7:5-6. The law did not really lead to righteousness. In fact, the law stirred up our sinful passions and produced more sin that eventually leads to death (bound to death). But now (7:6) because of His death, we are released from the law. We still serve God but not by a system of rules and regulations. Now we serve God by the Spirit that lives in us (the grace of God) and produces fruit; fruit toward life. We are on the trail, and we are headed in the right direction, feeling the effects of the Son on our face!

Circle the phrase, **Is the law sin?** *(7:7) and* **the law is holy** *(7:12). Highlight the phrase* **through the commandment sin might become utterly sinful** *(7:13).*

Is the Law Sinful?

Paul continued his series of questions (6:1, 14) with a question that arose out of the preceding illustration. If the law is what bound me to sin, is the law itself sinful? Paul's answer again was a definite no! Paul used a hypothetical illustration of the role of the law, a role he had already taught in Romans 2 and 3. Let's picture Paul saying it this way:

Imagine I was filled with covetousness (7:7). I couldn't take my eyes off of your new house, the swimming pool in your back yard or your gorgeous wife! Before I knew anything about the command that says, thou shalt not covet, I was free to enjoy my covetous ways. However, once I was introduced to the law, I realized how sinful my covetousness was and I tried to stop coveting. The law was God's righteous standard and righteousness was required for life. But instead of my obedience to the law bringing me life, I found the law to be impossible to keep so it brought me death instead. It wasn't the law that put me to death, it was sin. The law is and always has been God's holy and righteous standard (7:12). However, because of sin in me, it cannot make me righteous, it can only show me how utterly sinful I am so that I fall at God's feet and beg for mercy and grace!

Now we may be reading this and thinking that it doesn't really apply to us. After all, how many of us are still trying to please God by obeying the Ten Commandments? We know we were saved by grace, not by works. I wonder though if the church hasn't replaced the Ten Commandments with a list of "rules for spirituality" by which we judge, condemn, and criticize ourselves and others. Having a daily quiet time, sharing the Gospel with others, generously giving toward the Kingdom of God, and faithful church attendance are all very good things. But have we made them the law? Do we get life out of obeying them and feel condemned when we let them slip? Do we look down on others who don't keep the "laws"? According to this passage, I am free from the law of daily quiet time. I don't have to have a daily quiet time to follow Christ, and I don't have to feel guilty because I didn't have my quiet time today. That being said, as I follow Christ, His grace through His Spirit in me produces a desire to spend time with Him. That desire may lead me to have a quiet time today. Actually it already did!

Questions to Ponder:

1. Put the explanation of Paul's illustration in your own words.

2. Do you see the fruit of righteousness flowing out of you?

3. Have I adopted another set of "laws" to live by instead of living in relationship with Christ?

Day 17

◆◆◆◆◆◆◆◆◆◆◆◆◆◆◆◆◆◆◆◆◆◆◆

So, Is the Law Sin?
(Romans 7:14-25)

14 We know that the law is spiritual; but I am unspiritual, sold as a slave to sin. 15 I do not understand what I do. For what I want to do I do not do, but what I hate I do. 16 And if I do what I do not want to do, I agree that the law is good. 17 As it is, it is no longer I myself who do it, but it is sin living in me. 18 I know that nothing good lives in me, that is, in my flesh. For I have the desire to do what is good, but I cannot carry it out. 19 For what I do is not the good I want to do; no, the evil I do not want to do--this I keep on doing. 20 Now if I do what I do not want to do, it is no longer I who do it, but it is sin living in me that does it. 21 So I find this law at work: When I want to do good, evil is right there with me. 22 For in my inner being I delight in God's law; 23 but I see another law at work in the members of my body, waging war against the law of my mind and making me a prisoner of the law of sin at work within my members. 24 What a wretched man I am! Who will rescue me from this body of death? 25 Thanks be to God--through Jesus Christ our Lord! So then, I myself in my mind am a slave to God's law, but in the flesh a slave to the law of sin.

Years ago, I attended a men's retreat at Frontier Ranch in Buena Vista, Colorado. The Ranch is a Young Life Camp built on the side of Mt. Princeton towering 14,197 feet above sea level. As you can imagine, there are quite a few great hiking trails around the camp. I went with a group of men on one trail that led to a 120-foot cliff. On top of the cliff they had built a platform. As I stood at the bottom of the cliff, I knew there was no way in the world I would be able to climb it because it was so steep. But Frontier Ranch made a provision for me. They had ropes anchored at the platform that would allow you to climb up the cliff, much like a climbing wall at an amusement park, but this was the real thing. I was standing at the bottom of this cliff, with the provision necessary to climb it. The problem is that I had no desire in me to do so.

In the second half of Romans 7, Paul continued his personal illustration showing that though the law was righteous, it could not produce righteousness or life in us. It was as if Paul were standing at the bottom of the cliff of righteousness. Unlike me, he had the desire to climb this cliff (7:18), but he lacked the ability to follow through (7:18).

---

*Highlight the phrases **sold as a slave to sin** (7:14) and **rescue me from this body of death** (7:24).*

This passage is often used to illustrate the way a believer struggles against sin. However, in order to interpret it that way, we would have to ignore several important facts about the passage. First, it was the continuation of Paul's illustration that he began in 7:7 in which he described his life under the law, and his struggle with covetousness. He identified himself as a slave to sin (7:14). He had spent so much time teaching through Romans 6 that we are no longer slaves to sin (6:18) and that we are dead to sin (6:11). He would never confuse them by stating that now, as a believer, he was a slave to the desire of sin in him. He also asked who would rescue him from this death (7:24). His conclusion in Romans 6 was that the law leads to sin and death and the grace of God leads to righteousness and life. It is clear that Paul was continuing the illustration in which he was still struggling under the law to be righteous. So this is NOT the struggle of a Christian against sin. It is the agony of a person enslaved to sin who has a desire to do good and/or break the power of a sinful pattern but has not ability to do so. Striving to obey is exhausting which is why Jesus came to give us rest (Matthew 11:28).

---

*Underline the phrases **the law is good** (7:16), **nothing good lives in me** (7:17) and **desire to do what is good** (7:18). Circle the phrase **sin living in me** in 7:17 & 20.*

Striving Against Sin

In 7:15-20 Paul described the inner struggle of a person trying to live up to the righteous standard of the law. There is something about the righteous law that connects with a desire for obedience. This desire is a part of the image of God in us from the creation. This image is overshadowed by the presence of sin but the moral compass remains deep inside. Notwithstanding this desire, we try to connect this good desire with something good in us so that we can carry out the obedience, but we find nothing good (18). Finding nothing good to empower the desire, we naturally give in to the sin that lives in us (19). This would be like me standing at the foot of the cliff with a desire to ascend to the platform above but with no ability to do so. In Romans 1-3, Paul taught us that we are sinners to the core, none righteous, none who seek after God. This sin is dwelling in us body, soul, and spirit and ends up trumping our desire to do good (19). This illustration helped answer the question Paul asked in 7:7, *Is the law sin*? The law is not sin, it simply reveals and even magnifies the sin. Obviously according to this illustration, sin lives in us and makes it impossible for us to obey the law. It is interesting to note that Paul makes a distinction between us and our sin. I want to do good things, but the sin in me doesn't. Sin is not part of the real me, the me that God created, the me that has become a new creation in Christ!

Every New Year, we make resolutions. We are going to lose weight, we are going to exercise, we are going to control our anger, etc. Most of the time, the resolutions end up being good intentions. We give in to the desire to have another donut, sleep in, or blow up. In the end, we hate the resolutions and, after a time, we make disparaging remarks about resolutions in general. Are the resolutions evil? No, they appear evil because they seem to condemn us. The real evil is the lack of discipline inside of us. In the same way, Paul let us know that the law is not evil, but it does condemn us.

> *Put a box around the phrases **in my inner being** (7:22), **in the members of my body** (7:23) and **law of my mind** (7:23).*

Rescue

This struggle against sin before salvation involved our spirit (inner being) which is our true self, our flesh (members of my body), and our mind. We were sinners at the core of our being, it was our identity. The law of sin living in us was waging a war against our minds (23). It was convincing us that our fleshly desires were the most important and must be satisfied. This mindset drove our behavior and kept us prisoners because our flesh could never be satisfied, always desiring more. But for believers, this is no longer the case. We received a new spirit, the Holy Spirit of God, that has given us a whole new identity as saints, not sinners. The driver of our lives is no longer sin, so we are no longer in bondage to it. However, we did not receive a new body or a new mind. We renew our minds with the truth of our new identity, and we submit our bodies to the righteousness of God. This is the ongoing struggle of the believer, but it is not bondage.

When Paul asked the question, "who will rescue me", he answers with God, through Jesus Christ our Lord (7:25). He became sin and sin died in His body so that we could be raised to a new life and a new identity, free from sin! Righteous!

Questions to Ponder:
1. How do we know that Romans 7 is not depicting a Christian struggle with temptation?

2. What role does desire play in our obedience/disobedience?

3. The first paragraph under the title RESCUE is a summary of the Christian life. Put this in your own words.

Day 18

••••••••••••••••••••••

Relax!
(Romans 8:1-11)

*1 Therefore, there is now no condemnation for those who are in
Christ Jesus, 2 because through Christ Jesus the law of the Spirit
of life set me free from the law of sin and death. 3 For what the law
was powerless to do in that it was weakened by the flesh, God did
by sending his own Son in the likeness of sinful man to be a sin
offering. And so he condemned sin in sinful man, 4 in order that
the righteous requirements of the law might be fully met in us, who
do not live according to the flesh but according to the Spirit. 5
Those who live according to the flesh have their minds set on what
the flesh desires; but those who live in accordance with the Spirit
have their minds set on what the Spirit desires. 6 The mind of sinful
man is death, but the mind controlled by the Spirit is life and
peace; 7 the sinful mind is hostile to God. It does not submit to
God's law, nor can it do so. 8 Those controlled by the flesh cannot
please God.*

Years ago, I helped chaperone a group of high school seniors on a
five-day wilderness canoe trip through the boundary waters of
Canada north of Minnesota. We met with a guide to map out our
route, identify our campsites and estimate our arrival at the pick-up
point five days later. The trail was a combination of paddling
across lakes and then portaging our canoes, backpacks, etc.,
through the woods to the next lake. The map and schedule dictated
our day. We only had so much time to get to the next camp site,
and it was imperative that we do so before dark. This schedule put
us under law. We felt the pressure of time and distance to the next
location and, at some points, became frantic about moving the
team forward faster in order to keep up with the schedule. One
day, however, we had planned to simply stay at the camp site and
fish for the day. The spirit of the group was markedly different on
that day. There was no pressure, there was no law, and there was

no deadline to meet. We could rest, relax, and enjoy life! In Romans 8, Paul shares that we have been released from the pressure to perform; be more, do more, and keep up. We can relax.

---

*Circle the word **therefore** (8:1). Highlight in the same color the phrases **no condemnation** (8:1) and **he condemned sin** (8:3). Put a box around the phrase **in Christ Jesus** (8:1) and **law was powerless to do** (8:3).*

A Conclusion

Sometimes the chapter headings in our Bible can hinder our ability to see the flow of writing. Romans 8 begins with the word "therefore" and obviously introduces some kind of a conclusion. Our natural tendency would be to assume Paul is introducing the conclusion to the discussion in Romans 7 about whether or not the law is sin (7:7). However, the topic of no condemnation (8:1) seems to address a larger issue than the issue of the law. I believe that Paul is actually drawing some conclusions from his entire discussion beginning in Romans 1.

Paul began by introducing the concept of a Gospel that reveals a righteousness that comes by faith (1:17). In order to show us we all needed this righteousness, he began a lengthy discussion of the wrath (judgment or condemnation) of God that was going to be poured out on all unrighteousness (1:18). After convincing us that all of us are unrighteous (3:10), he assures us no one will be made righteous and escape God's wrath by obeying the law (3:20). We can, however, become righteous by faith in Jesus Christ (3:22). He then addressed the problem of sin in the life of the believer (Romans 6, 7) , assuring us we are dead to sin (6:11), no longer serve sin as our master (6:14), and are dead to the judgment that comes by the law (7:4). This brings us to Romans 8. Because of all of this, the wrath that is being revealed from Heaven (1:18) will NOT fall upon us as believers (8:1).

No condemnation, no fear of judgment, no wrathful angry God to face one day… this is good news (can you say Gospel?). *No condemnation* shuts down all preaching and teaching that is designed to produce blame, shame, or guilt in us. These are no longer our motivations. We don't have to behave so that we can escape God's wrath. Let's just sit with that a moment. Relax. Heavy sigh. We don't have to strive to stop sinning, we don't have to frantically serve God to counteract our weakness, and we don't have to feel driven to please God. He isn't waiting for us to do more or be more for Him… we can rest. How many times have we left a church service feeling if we only prayed more, our lives would be more blessed. If we could just bring ourselves to tithe, God would take care of all of our financial needs. If we were more disciplined with our eating habits, we could feel the love of God in deeper ways. This kind of thinking produces striving, which is flesh. Hebrews 4 tells of a Sabbath rest God had in mind for His people. Jesus invited the religious of His day to come to Him and rest (Matthew 11:28). He urged His followers simply to abide in Him (John 15:1). As if being made righteous wasn't enough good news, now we find we don't have to fear God's wrath either, we can stop striving and rest in His righteousness because it is enough. It just keeps getting better.

Paul reminds us that we are escaping wrath, not because of obedience to the law (it was powerless to accomplish this, 8:3), but because we are in Christ. It is not our behavior that keeps us from wrath, it is our location. When we received Christ by faith, we were placed into Christ by His Spirit. In Christ we died to sin, were buried, and have been raised again to a new life (6:4). The law brought sin and death, but the Spirit of God that placed us into Christ has set us free from sin and death (8:2).

What happened, then, to the wrath of God that was being revealed from Heaven against unrighteousness (1:18)? Did God simply overlook the sin and decide not to be angry about it? No, He chose to pour out all of His wrath upon Jesus on the cross. When Jesus took our sin and became our sin offering (8:3), he actually took the condemnation for my sin and condemned it (8:3). The cross proves God does not take a light view of sin. We have already seen that grace does not encourage sin. Sin caused God great pain in the death of His Son, the sacrifice for our sin.

Highlight in the same color the phrases **mind set on what the flesh desires** *(8:5),* **death** *(8:6),* **hostile to God** *(8:7),* **does not submit to God's law** *(8:7) and* **cannot please God** *(8:8). In another color highlight the phrases* **minds set on what the Spirit desires** *(8:5) and* **life and peace** *(8:6).*

Two Kinds of People

Since Christ took the condemnation for our sin, we no longer live out of our flesh; we now live out of the Spirit of God that lives in us. The Spirit can live in us because in Christ the righteous standard of God (the law) has been satisfied (8:4). This, then, separates us into one of two groups. We are either still living out of our flesh because our unrighteousness prevents the Spirit from entering, or we live out of the Spirit because Christ has made us righteous.

Romans 8:5-8 is not contrasting two types of believers, those who live in the flesh and those who live in the Spirit. It is contrasting two types of people, believers and unbelievers. Unbelievers live out of their flesh, think fleshly thoughts, follow fleshly desires, are still separated from God and are unable, despite their best efforts, to do anything that is pleasing to Him because nothing short of perfect righteousness pleases God. This way of life leads to death (8:5) which is separation from God. Believers live out of the Spirit, are motivated by Spiritual desire, and experience life (connection to God) and peace (settled relationship with Him) and are pleasing to God because they have received the perfect righteousness of Christ by faith. Remember the circle charts from Day 16? Those who live in the flesh have the flesh at their core. Those who live in the Spirit have the Spirit at their core. These are the only two types of people.

While it is true that our mind and flesh can still be at war with sin, the core of our being, the ruling factor, is either the flesh (for the unbeliever) or the Spirit (for the believer). This is confirmed by several phrases that Paul used in the passage. In 8:4 he said that those who have been made righteous *do not live according to the flesh but according to the Spirit*. He did not say should not or might not. He says do not! Then in 8:9, he emphatically stated we are not controlled by the flesh if the Spirit of God lives in us! This does not mean that we will not struggle with sin or flesh. The next passage will touch on that struggle. However, the point of this passage is that we are NOT under condemnation and we are NOT slaves to our flesh. It just keeps getting better!

Questions to Ponder:

1. How do you respond to the idea of simply resting in the finished work of Christ?

2. How does the cross illustrate God's attitude toward sin and toward us?

3. What is the difference between living out of the flesh and living out of the Spirit?

Day 19

◆◆◆◆◆◆◆◆◆◆◆◆◆◆◆◆◆◆◆◆◆◆◆◆

The Spirit is HERE!
(Romans 8:9-16)

9 You, however, are not in the flesh but in the Spirit, if the Spirit of God lives in you. And if anyone does not have the Spirit of Christ, he does not belong to Christ. 10 But if Christ is in you, your body is dead because of sin, yet your spirit is alive because of righteousness. 11 And if the Spirit of him who raised Jesus from the dead is living in you, he who raised Christ from the dead will also give life to your mortal bodies through his Spirit, who lives in you. 12 Therefore, brothers, we have an obligation--but it is not to the flesh, to live according to it. 13 For if you live according to the flesh, you will die; but if by the Spirit you put to death the misdeeds of the body, you will live, 14 because those who are led by the Spirit of God are sons of God. 15 For you did not receive a spirit that makes you a slave again to fear, but you received the Spirit of sonship. And by him we cry, ""Abba," Father." 16 The Spirit himself testifies with our spirit that we are God's children.

Imagine you are going on a hike with two of your friends. One of them is passionate about nature. He studies plants, animals, and habitats and has all of the latest hiking and camping gear. The other is a video game aficionado. He has every gaming system known to man and spends hours each day on the couch working his fingers to the bone. The first friend needs no encouragement along the hike. The passion inside of him drives him and interprets his experience as fun and pleasurable. The other friend needs constant encouragement from sources outside of himself because there is nothing in him that connects with this experience. The good news for us as believers is that we have something (or Someone) in us that drives us forward on our Christian journey. Can you identify ways that the Spirit has urged you forward?

Circle every occurrence of the word **spirit** in these verses

The Spirit is in Us!

The word "spirit" occurs 22 times in the book of Romans; 15 of those are found in Romans 8, and 12 in this short passage. I would say that this section is about the Spirit. In 9 of those 12 occurrences, the word spirit is referring to the Holy Spirit of God. He is called both the Spirit of God and the Spirit of Christ (8:9). The Spirit of God lives in us (8:9) and Christ is in us (8:10). Christ dwells in the believer through the Spirit, they are not separate but one. Paul had introduced the concept of living in the Spirit as opposed to living in the flesh earlier in this chapter (8:5-6) but now teaches truth about living in the Spirit.

Underline **in the Spirit** *(8:9),* **does not have** *and* **does not belong** *(8:9),* **your spirit is alive because of righteousness** *(8:10),* **give life to our mortal bodies** *(8:11),* **by the spirit you put to death the misdeeds of the body** *(8:13),* **led by the Spirit** *(8:14),* **Spirit of sonship** *(8:15)* **and testifies with our spirit** *(8:16).*

The Spirit is Active in Us

It is not hard to see after the first reading through this passage that God's Spirit is active in the life of the believer. Life in Christ is life in the Spirit, and Paul wants us to know what that looks like. He made a series of statements that teaches us how the presence of the Spirit in our lives affects us.

Paul began with an emphatic statement to all believers. In the previous verses, he told us that the flesh leads to death while the Spirit leads to life and peace (8:6). Then he told us that we are not in the flesh, we are in the Spirit. He doesn't say we should not live in the flesh or that we should strive to be in the Spirit. He says that we are NOT in the flesh but we ARE in the Spirit (8:9). When we received Christ by faith, the gift of His righteousness made us right in every way. At the core of our being, we came alive by the Spirit, and now that living Spirit is the core of our being. He is in the driver's seat, put there by God Himself and the flesh no longer has ruling power over us. The presence of the Spirit in us changes our location. We are no longer in the flesh, we are no longer in Adam, we are no longer in sin. We are NOW in Christ; we now live in the Spirit.

And Paul said these are the only two options. We are either in the flesh or in the Spirit. In fact if we don't have the Spirit in us, if we are not in Christ and in possession of His indwelling Spirit, we do not belong to Christ and are in the flesh (8:9). We are either in the Spirit or in the flesh. Period.

Paul had said that living in the Spirit was life and peace (8:6). He connected the righteousness or rightness that comes as a free gift with life. Christ's Spirit makes us alive because of righteousness (8:10). We were cut off from the source of life by sin and so were dead. Christ died for our sin and made us righteous. When we became right, His Spirit was able to come into our now righteous bodies and re-connect our spirit with the source of life so that our spirit comes alive. When we became righteous in Christ, we also came alive in Christ. This is what Christ came to do; give us life (John 10:10). God doesn't just see us as righteous or alive by looking through the rose colored glasses of Jesus, He has made us righteous and alive through Christ (His Spirit) in us.. It is now who we are!

He gave life to our spirit, but our bodies were unchanged and remained dead and disconnected from God, subject to the process of death and headed in that direction (8:10). Our bodies have developed patterns that cater to our own comfort. My sexual desire, love for cheesecake and quick wit do not always lead me in the direction of life. Am I a slave to these patterns? NO! Because the Spirit is life in me, it can have an affect on my body (8:11). We can choose to live the life of the Spirit out through our bodies and experience the life God always meant for us to live. The Spirit has power over our body. In Philippians, Paul taught that we are working out our salvation (Philippians 2:13). What does that mean? In Christ life and righteousness are at the core of who we are. However, we must choose to live out that true identity through our flesh. The power of the Spirit in us, the Spirit that made us alive can empower us to deny the sin that dwells in our bodies. Not only that, but it is that same Spirit that will raise up our dead, sinful, decaying bodies on the day of the resurrection. He is all about life; life now and life forever! Praise God for His Spirit in us!

Because the Spirit of God lives in every believer, He is active in every believer. Paul said that if we are children of God, we are being led by His Spirit (8:14). Jesus had predicted that the Spirit's role would be a role of guidance (John 16:13). He is always active in us, leading us toward truth. This is not just for those in ministry or those who spend hours each day in prayer and fasting. In Christ we all have the Spirit, we are all righteous, we are all alive, and we are all being led by His Spirit. Of course, we have a choice as to whether we follow His leading or not, but His desire is that we cooperate with the leading of the Spirit in us. It is a question of surrender.

The Spirit is Relational

This Spirit that is in us is not an impersonal force. On the contrary, He is all about relationship. He is called the Spirit of sonship. The Spirit in us reconnects us to the Father as His beloved children. Not only that, but the Spirit cultivates in us a relationship of intimacy that allows our hearts to cry out to the Father in an intimate way. *Abba* (8:5) is a term of intimacy akin to our English word "daddy." The Spirit connects us to the heart of the Father in such a way that we desire more and more of Him. Prayer, meditation, quiet time, corporate worship, and Bible study are not rules that we obey in order to get close to God. They are the expression of the Spirit that lives in us and leads us into deeper intimacy with the Father. The Spirit connects us to the deeper desire of intimacy with God.

Doubt is a tool of Satan used to try to disconnect us intellectually and emotionally from the Father. He caused Eve to doubt in the garden, he caused Peter to doubt when he was standing at the campfire during the trial of Jesus and he wants to make us doubt our true identity. He accuses us night and day (Revelation 12:10) and even builds up strongholds of lies that exalt themselves above the truth of God in our lives (II Corinthians 10:4-5). But the Holy Spirit in us reminds us of the truth of who we are in Christ and confirms the fact that we are children of the Father. This reminder is vital, since our behavior tends to flow out of our identity. If I listen to the Spirit and believe I am righteous, alive, and a child of the Father, my behavior will reflect that belief. Satan is always on the prowl, so it is such a blessing to have the regular reminders from God through His Spirit.

In Ephesians, Paul instructs us that the Christian life is like a battle. Satan is the enemy and he uses deceit and lies to defeat us just like He did Eve in the Garden of Eden. However, we have been given the truth, the Sword of the Spirit, which is God's word (Ephesians 6:17). Knowing who we are is the greatest weapon we have and is powerful enough to defeat the lies of Satan that empower our flesh.

Paul had started this chapter by telling us that the Gospel just keeps getting better, including the fact that there is no condemnation for us. In this passage he shared the benefits of having the Spirit of Christ living in us. It does just keep getting better. What a glorious gospel!

Questions to Ponder:

1. In what ways is the Spirit of God active in the believer?

2. How does the Spirit affect our body?

3. What is the Spirit of Sonship?

Day 20

♦♦♦♦♦♦♦♦♦♦♦♦♦♦♦♦♦♦♦♦♦♦

Suffering and Glory
(Romans 8:17-27)

17 Now if we are children, then we are heirs--heirs of God and co-heirs with Christ, if indeed we share in his sufferings in order that we may also share in his glory 18 I consider that our present sufferings are not worth comparing with the glory that will be revealed in us. 19 The creation waits in eager expectation for the sons of God to be revealed. 20 For the creation was subjected to frustration, not by its own choice, but by the will of the one who subjected it, in hope 21 that the creation itself will be liberated from its bondage to decay and brought into the glorious freedom of the children of God. 22 We know that the whole creation has been groaning as in the pains of childbirth right up to the present time. 23 Not only so, but we ourselves, who have the first fruits of the Spirit, groan inwardly as we wait eagerly for our adoption as sons, the redemption of our bodies. 24 For in this hope we were saved. But hope that is seen is no hope at all. Who hopes for what he already has? 25 But if we hope for what we do not yet have, we wait for it patiently. 26 In the same way, the Spirit helps us in our weakness. We do not know what we ought to pray for, but the Spirit himself intercedes for us with groans that words cannot express. 27 And he who searches our hearts knows the mind of the Spirit, because the Spirit intercedes for the saints in accordance with God's will.

In July 2012, the largest wildfire on record in New Mexico was burning through over 300,000 acres of forest in the Gila National Forest. Over 300 square miles of forest were destroyed by fire. Hiking through this section of the forest a year later creates a somber mood as the blackened tree stumps seem to stand in the fields like grave markers. However, amidst the black are tiny patches of green growth. These small saplings, wildflowers, and vines create a picture of hope for the future. One day, this forest will be beautiful again! Hiking through this trail brings a mixture of sadness for what has been lost and hope for the future.

Paul has convinced us all that we are sinners (Roman 1-3), told us about a wonderful gift of righteousness that is given apart from the law (Roman 4-5), and helped us understand our relationship to sin as a believer (Romans 6-7). Paul opened up Romans 8 by revealing the source of this new life of righteousness; it is the Spirit of God in us. He ended the first section by reminding us that the Spirit in us confirms our status as children of God (8:16)!

Now it is time for a reality check. Following the positive direction of Paul's words and the feeling that this just keeps getting better, we may become complacent and believe that we are now living on easy street. However, if your life is like mine, you would agree that easy street is not a good description of life as it is now. The passage builds on the concept of being God's child by including the fact that we are also God's heirs, which make us co-heirs with Christ (8:17). We get to share in His inheritance. That sounds great until we read that the inheritance includes both glory and suffering (8:17).

---

*Circle the words **sufferings** (8:18), **frustration** (8:20), **bondage to decay** (8:21), **groaning** (8:22), **groan inwardly** (8:23), **weakness** (8:26) and **groans** (8:26).*

Groaning

Being in Christ definitely has its perks. We get life, we get righteousness, we get freedom from death, freedom from sin, and freedom from the law. I told you it was good news! But, the reality is that being in Christ also means we get to share in His suffering (8:17). Jesus had told his disciples that the world would be difficult for them (John 16:33; John 15:18). Paul used the word "groan" to create a word picture of the suffering. The word he used is a word that means heavy sigh and is usually associated with grief.

Let's say you have been working on a project at work for two weeks and then the system crashes and you lose all of your work (heavy sigh). You have not been feeling well and go to the doctor to find that you have cancer (heavy sigh). The school principal calls to tell you that your son has been suspended for drug use (heavy sigh). The disappointments and difficulties of life make us groan.

Paul used the word groan three times. First the creation groans (8:20), then we groan (8:23), and finally the Spirit groans (8:26). These disappointments and difficulties come on the physical level, the personal level, and the spiritual level.

The creation is used as an illustration of suffering and groaning. Mankind's choice to sin and disobey God had an impact on the creation itself. The earth was cursed because of man (Genesis 3:17-19). Thorns, thistles, fear in the animal kingdom, natural disasters, parasites, etc., have limited the earth from bearing the kind of fruit it was created to produce. It is experiencing what Paul called frustration or failure to thrive (8:20) and has become subject to the law of entropy. Everything is in a constant state of decaying or dying (8:21).

We are groaning because though our spirits have come alive through Christ, our bodies are still mortal and subject to pain, sickness, and temptation. We sigh heavily every time we are reminded of our mortality, weakness, and limitations (8:23). Paul used the word "weakness" (8:26) to describe this. It means that we lack the capacity to understand, accomplish, or bear up under some thing in our lives. We can't slow the aging process, we can't always control our feelings and we can't stop other people from acts of terrorism or abuse, this is evidence of our weakness.

The Spirit of Christ that lives in us (8:11) groans along with us, interpreting our heavy sighs to the Father, because we can't seem to find the words to express what it is we really want or need. The Spirit is called the Comforter or *Paraclete*, one who comes alongside. In our weakness, we are not alone. God Himself, in the person of the Spirit, groans alongside us and interprets our groanings to the Father. So even the bad news has good news attached to it. We never groan alone. The Holy Spirit and I have regular groaning sessions. When I invite Him to groan with me, I always end up encouraged. When we groan inwardly without inviting the Holy Spirit, the groans have no resolution. We just keep telling ourselves that we don't know what to do or repeat the question "why" in our mind over and over again. These thoughts just keep spinning in our heads as dilemmas with no solution, creating anxiety and despair.

Underline the words **eager expectation** *(8:19),* **hope** *(8:20),* **wait eagerly** *(8:23),* **hope** *(8:24) and* **wait for it patiently** *(8:25).*

Hoping

Without the Spirit living in us, this groaning would lead to despair and discouragement. However, the presence of the Spirit of God is only the firstfruits of what God has in store for us. Under the Old Covenant, the Israelites brought the firstfruits of their harvest as an offering to God (Leviticus 23). It was a guarantee of what was to come. Christ is called the firstfruits from the dead (I Corinthians 15:23). His resurrection guarantees our resurrection. Paul said we have the firstfruits of the Spirit. The Spirit of God living in us is a guarantee of greater life ahead. So the groaning doesn't lead to despair, it leads to hope and the Spirit's abiding presence in us is a constant reminder of that hope.

The words *eager expectation* (8:19) are actually translated *standing on tiptoe* in the Phillips translation of the Bible. The creation is standing on its tiptoes leaning forward for the curse to be lifted. Paul used the word again in verse 23 to describe our attitude toward the redemption of our bodies. Our flesh continues to struggle with temptation, addiction, disobedience, sickness, pain, and death. We are eager to trade in these bodies for our perfect, glorified bodies (can I get an AMEN?).

This expectation of good creates hope in us. Hope is the confident and joyful expectation of good in the future. The good in the future that we are hoping for is the glory of God (8:17, 18). The Glory of God always marks His presence. The Glory of God hovered over the tabernacle in the wilderness, over the mercy seat in the temple, and around the angels announcing the birth of Jesus. We will share in the Glory of God. We will be eternally in His presence, with glorified bodies on a perfect planet with no decay, no weakness, and no groaning. In his sermon entitled *Weight of Glory*, C.S. Lewis says, "The door on which we have been knocking all of our lives will open at last." The groan turns into a shout of celebration and a sigh of relief.

So we have inherited the sufferings of Christ and the Glory of Christ. The good news is, while the sufferings might be difficult, they pale in comparison to the splendor of the glory which is our hope. John stated that we are currently the sons of God, but we don't yet see it fully (I John 3:2). Paul said in another epistle that our current troubles are actually moving us toward the Glory of God (II Corinthians 4:7). We keep our eyes fixed on the glory instead of the suffering, but we do allow a heavy sigh from time to time. It is okay to groan, and we don't groan alone.

Recently I heard a song entitled "Worn" by Tenth Avenue North. The lyrics express this tension between suffering and hope.

I'm Tired I'm worn
My heart is heavy
From the work it takes
To keep on breathing
I've made mistakes
I've let my hope fail
My soul feels crushed
By the weight of this world

And I know that you can give me rest
So I cry out with all that I have left

Let me see redemption win
Let me know the struggle ends
That you can mend a heart
That's frail and torn
I wanna know a song can rise
From the ashes of a broken life
And all that's dead inside can be reborn
Cause I'm worn

I know I need to lift my eyes up
But I'm too weak
Life just won't let up
And I know that you can give me rest
So I cry out with all that I have left

My prayers are wearing thin
Yeah, I'm worn
Even before the day begins
Yeah, I'm worn
I've lost my will to fight
I'm worn
So, heaven come and flood my eyes

Questions to Ponder:

1. What kind of things make you groan?

2. Do you invite the Holy Spirit to groan with you? Do you take
   your groanings to God? Or do you let them spin in your
   head?

3. Make a list of things you hope for in Christ.

Day 21

◆◆◆◆◆◆◆◆◆◆◆◆◆◆◆◆◆◆◆◆◆◆

Is This Trail Safe?
(Romans 8:28-39)

28 And we know that in all things God works for the good of those who love him, who have been called according to his purpose. 29 For those God foreknew he also predestined to be conformed to the likeness of his Son, that he might be the firstborn among many brothers. 30 And those he predestined, he also called; those he called, he also justified; those he justified, he also glorified. 31 What, then, shall we say in response to this? If God is for us, who can be against us? 32 He who did not spare his own Son, but gave him up for us all--how will he not also, along with him, graciously give us all things? 33 Who will bring any charge against those whom God has chosen? It is God who justifies. 34 Who is he that condemns? Christ Jesus, who died--more than that, who was raised to life--is at the right hand of God and is also interceding for us. 35 Who shall separate us from the love of Christ? Shall trouble or hardship or persecution or famine or nakedness or danger or sword? 36 As it is written: "For your sake we face death all day long; we are considered as sheep to be slaughtered." 37 No, in all these things we are more than conquerors through him who loved us. 38 For I am convinced that neither death nor life, neither angels nor demons, neither the present nor the future, nor any powers, 39 neither height nor depth, nor anything else in all creation, will be able to separate us from the love of God that is in Christ Jesus our Lord.

One day while on a retreat in the mountains of North Carolina, I decided to go on a hike. I had noticed a trail that began near the place I was staying. The trail ahead was wide, flat, and inviting. About an hour into the hike, the trail narrowed. On my left was a steep drop off to a ravine about 70 feet below. To my right was a cliff stretching up about 20 feet. There were some trees growing out the side of the cliff, with low branches that fell over the path. These branches were infested with spider webs. Also on the cliff side were small caves, crevices, and arrangements of rock that would easily house snakes. My inviting path had turned ominous. How could I continue to go forward, fearful of sliding down into the ravine, getting covered with spiders and spider webs, or getting bit by a snake?

This is exactly where we find ourselves in our hike through Romans. Paul began chapter eight with inviting words of freedom. The Spirit of the living God has entered into us by faith and freed us from the law, from sin, and from death. He even connected us with God in such a way that we become co-heirs with Christ! Woohoo! Then the path begins to narrow. This inheritance includes both glory and suffering. Wait a minute! We signed up for life, freedom, righteousness, glory... nobody said anything to us about suffering!

In the remainder of Romans 8, Paul assured us that in spite of the suffering, we are safe. He gives us three reasons:

1) God's plan (purpose) is sure (8:28-30).
2) God is for us, He is on our side (8:31-34).
3) God's love-bond with us is unbreakable (8:35-39).

There is so much information here, we are going to divide it into two days on your trail.

---

*Put a box around the words **all things** (28). Circle the words **according to his purpose** and put a capital A in front of the phrase. Underline the words **foreknew** (29), **predestined** (29), **called** (30), **justified** (30) and **glorified** (30) and number them one through five.*

God's Plan is Sure

God's plan or purpose is sure, and we will be safe in spite of all that might be happening. The promise in Romans 8:28 is referring to the suffering that Paul had been talking about in 8:18-27. It was hard to believe that this wonderful grace-filled Gospel of the gift of righteousness could include something as painful as suffering. Paul assured us in verse 28 that even these sufferings will work for the good of those that God has called, those who have received the Spirit (8:11) who confirms their calling (8:16). The question is what did he mean by good? Suffering never seems good to me, so Paul must have a different definition than I do! Since he says it will be good for those who are called according to His purpose, good would be defined by God's purpose. The word that is used for purpose here is a word which literally means to "set forth" or "place in view." It was used of the process of laying out the 12 loaves of showbread in the Jewish tabernacle/temple. God has placed in our view a plan or purpose, and everything that is happening in our lives is working toward good in relationship to this plan. What is the plan? The plan is described by a progression of five verbs, all in the aorist tense that indicates past action. These five actions have already been accomplished in us and reveal God's ultimate purpose for us.

The plan began with God's **foreknowledge** (29). There has been a lot of discussion about this verse in relationship to God knowing in advance who would go to Heaven and who would go to Hell. This verse, however, is not about WHAT God foreknew but WHO God foreknew. Of all of the possible human beings to be potentially born through the history of the world, God foreknew you would be a part of His plan or purpose. Since every male sperm is imprinted with a slightly different DNA pattern, the probability of you being born as distinctly "you" is about 1 in 200 million. Add to that the probability of you being exposed to the Gospel and choosing to believe, and it is absolutely amazing that God foreknew YOU! Since God operates outside of the time continuum, His foreknowledge and your choice could be considered simultaneous rather than causative. He didn't foreknow you BECAUSE you would choose and you didn't choose BECAUSE He foreknew you. The point is He foreknew YOU.

Now those he foreknew, he also **predestined** (29). This word is also misunderstood and used to teach that some are predestined to go to Heaven while others are predestined to go to Hell. But this verse is not about Heaven or Hell. It is addressed to people who are already believers and it involves the direction they are headed from here. God was revealing His goal for those who believe and that goal is to be conformed to the image of His Son. God's ultimate purpose for us is not that we would be happy, but that we would represent, reflect, and reveal Christ through our lives. God desires that we grow spiritually into the kind of person that loves, rejoices, shows compassion, speaks truth, and dispenses grace just like Jesus! This changes everything. If this is the goal, then what is good (8:28) would be anything that helps to develop that kind of character in us. Unfortunately, it is true that suffering is a key component in character development. So suffering is good because it helps us to exhibit the character of Christ. He didn't say it would feel good, he said it would work toward good.

If we are predestined to be conformed to the image of Christ, that implies that we have been **called.** The calling is the wooing of the Spirit of God that draws us to the Gospel and the free gift of righteousness. It is possible to resist this work of the Spirit, but ultimately if we are truly called, we will come to the Father through Jesus and receive the gift of the Spirit. Being called makes us one of God's elect (we will deal with that term in chapter 9). But again, God's calling does not cause our choice. Just as Israel was God's elect people under the Old Covenant, so the church is God's elect people under the New Covenant. We are "...a chosen people, a royal priesthood, a holy nation, a people belonging to God..." (I Peter 2:9). Later, Paul admonished the Ephesian Christians to make sure that their behavior and manner of life was consistent with their calling. In others words, live out your new identity in Christ as God's chosen ones. God's call on our lives extends past receiving the Gospel. The Spirit continues to call or woo us toward Christlike character and spiritual maturity.

As the elect called of God, we have been **justified** or declared righteous. This fits right in with Paul's theme through these first eight chapters. The Gospel introduces a righteousness that cannot be earned but is given as a free gift by faith. Believers are not being justified or earning righteousness. We are already justified and have been made to be as we were always meant to be; Righteous!. The final part of God's plan is **glorification**. As we discussed in the last chapter, the Glory of God marks His presence. When the righteousness and calling that are in us begins to be seen through us, it is the life of God through the Person of Christ that is being shown to the world. This is God's Glory!

So, God's purpose was to bring us to a place where our character is lived out in such a way that it brings glory to God. Every circumstance that God allows in our lives can be used by Him to move us further along that path, so it is good. When the circumstances of my life, even the suffering, ultimately brings glory to God, it is good. Therefore, we are not threatened by this suffering, we are comforted by it (though not always happy about it). We are safe!

Questions to Ponder:
1. List the progression of 5 words Paul uses in this passage and explain how they connect to each other.

2. Re-write this progression in a way that personalizes it for you.

3. What is the intended result of this progression?

Day 22

♦♦♦♦♦♦♦♦♦♦♦♦♦♦♦♦♦♦♦♦♦♦♦

Is This Trail Safe? (part 2)
(Romans 8:28-39)

28 And we know that in all things God works for the good of those who love him, who have been called according to his purpose. 29 For those God foreknew he also predestined to be conformed to the likeness of his Son, that he might be the firstborn among many brothers. 30 And those he predestined, he also called; those he called, he also justified; those he justified, he also glorified. 31 What, then, shall we say in response to this? If God is for us, who can be against us? 32 He who did not spare his own Son, but gave him up for us all--how will he not also, along with him, graciously give us all things? 33 Who will bring any charge against those whom God has chosen? It is God who justifies. 34 Who is he that condemns? Christ Jesus, who died--more than that, who was raised to life--is at the right hand of God and is also interceding for us. 35 Who shall separate us from the love of Christ? Shall trouble or hardship or persecution or famine or nakedness or danger or sword? 36 As it is written: "For your sake we face death all day long; we are considered as sheep to be slaughtered." 37 No, in all these things we are more than conquerors through him who loved us. 38 For I am convinced that neither death nor life, neither angels nor demons, neither the present nor the future, nor any powers, 39 neither height nor depth, nor anything else in all creation, will be able to separate us from the love of God that is in Christ Jesus our Lord.

As I continued down the trail in the mountains of North Carolina I must admit that the steep cliff, the narrow trail and the abundance of spider webs made me think about turning back (can't you hear me saying, *"ravines and spiders and snakes, oh my!"* However, with each step I took forward, I gained a confidence that I had what it takes to keep going. As we recognize what God has done for us and realize that He is with us and for us, our confidence grows as well.

> *Circle the words **If God is for us, who can be against us** (31) and put a capital B in front of the phrase. Underline the phrase, **did not spare his own son** (32) and write the word proof beside it. Underline the phrase, **graciously give us all things** (32) and write the word promise beside it. Underline the phrase, **also interceding for us** (34) and write the word protection beside it. Circle the words **all things** (32).*

God is For Us

Not only is God's plan sure but God is on our side. He is **for** us. Sometimes we begin to believe that all of the bad things that are happening to us are God's fault. The negative consequences of people's bad choices which affect us adversely did not originate with God. He is not up in heaven trying to see how difficult He can make our lives. Ray Stedman, who pastored in California in the 1970's (www.raystedman.org), shared a great story that illustrates this point. It seems that a grandson of someone in his church was Hispanic and moved with his family to an area where most of the population was Caucasian. He started school in his new neighborhood and was bullied and ridiculed for the color of his skin. He came home several days in a row crying, and his parents did not know what to do. This boy and his parents were Christians, so they prayed for God's protection. A few evenings later, a boy from the grandson's school came to their house. We will call him Mike. Mike was in the same grade but was twice the size of the boy. He introduced himself and told the family that he was a Christian. He came by because he heard they were Christians, and he wanted to promise to go to school the next day and tell everyone if they picked on this kid they would answer to him. In this situation, the boy was safe because Mike was **for** him. In the same way, we are up against an enemy that seeks to devour us, in a world that doesn't understand us or even hates us, and are surrounded by people who make poor choices that affect us regularly. But God is **for** us and He goes with us everywhere, everyday. We are safe!

It is easy to say that God is for us, but sometimes the negative circumstances that surround us seem to scream that God is against us, trying to get our attention, punish us, or even destroy us. Paul followed up the statement with proof. In two words, the proof is: **remember Jesus**. Our value to God is communicated by the price He was willing to pay for us. He paid the greatest price, the life of His only Son Jesus. He has forever proven, in spite of any current negative circumstances, that He is for us.

Paul followed the proof with a promise. Not only is God NOT the author of these negative circumstances, it is His desire to give us good things. We have already alluded to the fact that this Gospel just keeps getting better and better. In the midst of suffering, it is important to focus on the Heart of God for us. He wants to give us good things, things that match the gift He has already given us, things that lead to life, things that are for our good. These things include experiencing love, joy and peace (Galatians 5:22-23).

However, He doesn't promise to take the negative circumstances away. He doesn't necessarily end all of the suffering. He does, however, promise that Jesus is always in His presence interceding on our behalf. Satan accuses us (Revelation 12:10), and Jesus defends us! The closing arguments should be intense, but we know who wins. This reminds me of Jesus' conversation with Peter in Luke 22 where Jesus told Peter that Satan had a plan for his life; he wanted to sift him like wheat (a rigorous process). Jesus followed the bad news with comforting news. He promised Peter that He, Jesus, the Son of God, was praying for him. Paul is telling us that Jesus is having the same conversation with us that He had with Peter. Yes, Satan is attacking, the world is pressing in, suffering hurts, we are being sifted like wheat but Jesus is praying for us. Whew! What a relief!

> *Circle the words **who shall separate us from the love of Christ**
> (35) and put a capital C in front of the phrase. Draw a heart over
> the word **love or loved** (35, 37, 39). Underline the phrase **more
> than conquerors** (38). Circle the word **all these things** (37).*

God's Love Bond is Unbreakable

Paul closed out this passage by focusing on the bond that exists
between us and God through our faith in Christ. It is not a bond of
duty. It is not a bond of obedience to the law. It is a bond of love.
It is the love of Christ, proven at the cross and shed abroad in our
hearts through His Spirit that lives in us (Romans 5:5). He
acknowledged the severity of the trouble by stating that *we face
death all day long* (36), but said emphatically that there is
absolutely nothing that can break this bond of love that exists
between God and us. We could take the time to analyze every
particular thing that Paul mentioned, but the bigger point is that
nothing can separate us. Let's make our own list. Unfaithful
spouses, life-threatening illness, job layoffs, rebellious children,
death of a loved one, financial ruin, sinful addictions, poor choices,
tornados, hurricanes, nor tsunamis can change the fact that we are
safe in the arms of a loving Father. We can count on it.

Whatever circumstance or trial that tempts you to believe God
doesn't love you can be inserted into this list. Go ahead, write it in
right after the word *depth* in verse 39. Read it out loud...no...
proclaim it out loud. You are safe!

Not only that, but these things that seem to threaten our bond with
God don't stand a chance. God's love not only overcomes them, it
provides us with an overwhelming victory. We aren't just
conquerors, we are more than conquerors (37).

This trek through Romans 8 had gotten a little scary, but at this
point, we can march forward on the path with confidence and
assurance, knowing that we are deeply, eternally and
unconditionally loved!

Questions to Ponder:

1. How would knowing that God is for you change the way you
   face certain negative circumstances?

2. Imagine Jesus saying to you what he said to Peter in Luke
   22. How would you respond?

3. What kinds of things make you 'feel' like God doesn't love
   you? How can you overcome those feelings?

Day 23

♦♦♦♦♦♦♦♦♦♦♦♦♦♦♦♦♦♦♦♦♦♦♦♦

Let God Be God
(Romans 9:1-13)

1 I speak the truth in Christ--I am not lying, my conscience confirms it in the Holy Spirit-- 2 I have great sorrow and unceasing anguish in my heart. 3 For I could wish that I myself were cursed and cut off from Christ for the sake of my brothers, those of my own race, 4 the people of Israel. Theirs is the adoption as sons; theirs the divine glory, the covenants, the receiving of the law, the temple worship and the promises. 5 Theirs are the patriarchs, and from them is traced the human ancestry of Christ, who is God over all, forever praised! Amen. 6 It is not as though God's word had failed. For not all who are descended from Israel are Israel. 7 Nor because they are his descendants are they all Abraham's children. On the contrary, "It is through Isaac that your offspring will be reckoned." 8 In other words, it is not the natural children who are God's children, but it is the children of the promise who are regarded as Abraham's offspring. 9 For this was how the promise was stated: "At the appointed time I will return, and Sarah will have a son." 10 Not only that, but Rebekah's children had one and the same father, our father Isaac. 11 Yet, before the twins were born or had done anything good or bad--in order that God's purpose in election might stand: 12 not by works but by him who calls--she was told, "The older will serve the younger." 13 Just as it is written: "Jacob I loved, but Esau I hated."

In the first Jurassic Park movie, Paleontologist Dr. Grant finds himself hiking through a jungle filled with vicious dinosaurs. He is accompanied by his assistant, Dr. Sattler, the owners' grandchildren, Tim and Lex, and the owners' lawyer Donald. When they find themselves in danger, it becomes quickly apparent that Donald has no compassion for the children and thinks only of himself. Dr. Grant on the other hand, is willing to sacrifice his life for the children. This is the kind of leader I want to take me through the jungle!

The Apostle Paul has been our guide through the dangerous theological jungle of Romans. There have already been many controversial truths, truths that particularly upset the mind and heart of those of Jewish descent. As Paul transitions to Romans 9, he wants to share his heart for the Jews in the middle of this jungle because the trail isn't going to be getting any easier.

> *Number the following words on phrases in verses 4-5. 1 adoption of sons, 2 divine glory, 3 covenants, 4 receiving the law, 5 temple worship, 6 promises, 7 patriarchs and 8 human ancestry of Christ.*

Affirmation of the Jewish People

As we have journeyed through Romans 1-8, it seems that Paul had been hard on the Jewish people. He had taken away any confidence they may have had in their status and basically told them that now they were on equal footing with the Gentiles in the eyes of God. That was a hard pill for them to swallow. Paul was getting ready to introduce an even harder concept in Romans 9, the concept of predestination or election. This was going to be another difficult truth for the Jewish people. Paul felt it necessary to share his heart for Israel before he moved on.

In 9:1-3, Paul declared that he would willingly sacrifice not only his life, but his eternal destiny, if he could see his race, his people (Israel), come to faith. You may have a loved one who doesn't know Christ. Sometimes, in speaking to them, you may come across as judgmental and harsh (because the Gospel is exclusive and truth is truth). Sprinkled in between those times of speaking truth, there needs to be a background of love and compassion. Paul revealed his feelings concerning the Jewish people. His words were poignant and emphatic. He spoke truth, not lying, confirmed by his own conscience and the Holy Spirit in him.

Not only did Paul want the Jews to know the depth of his concern for them, he also wanted to affirm or validate their esteemed past. They were considered God's chosen people in the Old Testament. The children of Israel were called the children of God; they had been adopted into His family. As they travelled through the wilderness or worshipped in the temple, they were able to see the Shekinah glory of God that marked His presence. They had been the recipients of covenants or special contracts with God through people like Abraham, Moses, and David. They alone had been given God's law, a reflection of His righteousness. They were called regularly to come and worship Him at His temple which was one of the most beautiful buildings in the world. They were given great promises. A Jewish descendant would bless the whole world, rule on the throne, and usher in the Kingdom of God. The patriarchs, Abraham, Isaac and Jacob, revered by all, were Jewish. Finally, the very message of salvation by faith was introduced through one of their own, Jesus of Nazareth. None of these things were negated by the Gospel; in fact, they were all preludes to the Gospel!

---

*Put a question mark over the word **failed** (6). Highlight the phrase **for not all who are descended from Israel are Israel** (6). Circle the word **Isaac** (7) and the words **children of promise** (8) and draw a line connecting the two. Circle the words **Rebekah's children** (10), **same father** (10) and **not by works** (12) and draw a line connecting all three.*

Who Are God's Chosen People?

Nothing in this next section (6-13) will make sense if we don't understand the historical context. Abraham is considered the father of the Jews. God called him out of the heathen nations and promised that he would make him a great nation (Genesis 12). As years went on, Abraham and his wife Sarah had no children and they began to doubt God's promise. They made a plan to produce their own heir by sending Hagar, Sarah's handmaid, into Abraham. Hagar conceived and bore a son named Ishmael. Ishmael was a descendant of Abraham, but he was born out of a fleshly plan and not as a result of faith in God's promise. Finally, when it was physically impossible, God fulfilled his promise to Abraham and Sarah and gave them a son, Isaac. Isaac is both a descendant of Abraham and the son of promise. Isaac married Rebekah and they had twin sons, Jacob and Esau. While the boys were still in the womb, God declared that Jacob, the younger, would rule over Esau, the older. This choice God made was not made based on their heritage, because they both had the same heritage. It was not based on their works or behavior, because they hadn't even been born yet. It was a choice made by God to fulfill His ultimate purposes. Jacob's name was later changed to Israel and he was the father of 12 boys who became the leaders of the 12 tribes of Israel. Paul's point was that not everyone who was a physical descendant of Abraham was part of Israel (the Jewish nation). Not everyone who descended from Israel (Jacob) was a part of Israel (God's chosen). From the beginning God intended for His Chosen People to be made up of both Jews and Gentiles. Hadn't He said that through Abraham *every* nation of the world would be blessed? This is the point of Paul's discussion here. He is pointing out that it has always been God's plan to include the Gentiles by faith. He finally gets to this conclusion later in the chapter (9:30, 31).

Now that we understand the history and the point Paul was making, we can understand the passage better. Paul had just told how important Israel was to God and to him (9:1-5). Since Israel did not embrace Christ or the Gospel, a valid question might arise in our minds; was God's "Israel project" a failure (6)? Of course the answer is no. The next verse explains why it was not a failure. Look at the phrase we highlighted in verse 6, *for not all who are descended from Israel are Israel.* All of the advantages listed in verses 4-5 were given to the physical descendants of Abraham. But God does not consider the true Israel, His chosen ones, His sons, and daughters to be merely physical descendants. If God's chosen ones were physical descendants, the family of Ishmael would have to be included in God's chosen nation. Ishmael was not a part of God's Israel, because he represented flesh and man's effort. Isaac, on the other hand, was the son of promise and was the fruit of Abraham's faith. The children of God are the children of promise or those who have faith in God. Paul taught this same truth to the churches of Galatia:

"If you belong to Christ, then you are Abraham's seed, and heirs according to the promise." (Galatians 3:29)

Even in the Old Covenant, it was really always about faith. God reprimanded His people for going through all of the motions of the Jewish religion but not coming to Him with their heart, their innermost being (Isaiah 29:13). Not only that, but God always had in mind to include the Gentile world in His Kingdom. His sovereign choices throughout the Old Testament may seem unfair to us, but He was working a greater plan. We cannot comprehend His ways (Romans 11:33).

God's Sovereign Choices

Paul moved to the next generation to further illustrate His point. When Rebekah was pregnant with twin sons, Jacob and Esau, God chose Jacob to be the one through whom the promises to Abraham would be fulfilled. God chose Jacob over Esau even though they both had the same heritage and neither had demonstrated any faith in the promise at all. Paul's point was that God has THE plan and He has the authority to make choices consistent with that plan, because He is God! God always had a plan and His sovereign choices were made with that plan in mind. His choice of Jacob may seem unfair to us. Actually, it was fair for Him to choose neither. Mankind had willingly sinned against Him and deserved nothing but death. God's choice of Jacob was not unfair, it was grace. Not only that, but through His choice of Jacob, the descendants of Esau are included in the Kingdom of God, as are the descendants of Ishmael, if they put their faith in the promised One.

So what about the phrase stating that God hated Esau (13)? Paul was using the word in the same sense that Jesus used it in Luke 14:26. In that verse, we were instructed to hate our parents in order to follow Jesus. It is a comparative term and simply pictures choosing one over another.

Often, this passage in Romans 9 is used to teach the doctrine of election or predestination. If we keep the passage in context, Paul was not talking about choosing some to go to Heaven and some to go to Hell. He was talking about choosing one to be a part of God's plan for redemption and not the other. This whole discussion was written in the context of showing the grace of God in extending righteousness by faith to the Gentiles. His sovereign choice was not about excluding, it was about including and it's not about individuals, it's about nations. God's selection of Jacob to be the channel through which His plan would be worked did not exclude Esau from righteousness, it offered righteousness to all through the plan.

Are we willing to let God be God? Are we willing to trust His choices even when they don't make sense to us? God knows that some circumstances seem to say that God is against us. This was true of the Israelites throughout their history. God instituted the Jewish feasts to remind them that God had been faithful in the past, even if it didn't seem like it in the present. We can count on Him, on His promise – by faith.

Questions to Ponder:

1. What is the main teaching of this passage that must be kept in mind when interpreting what is said?

2. According to this passage, who is Israel?

3. Explain how God's choices are NOT unfair.

Day 24

♦♦♦♦♦♦♦♦♦♦♦♦♦♦♦♦♦♦♦♦♦♦♦

Is God Unfair?
(Romans 9:14-33)

14 What then shall we say? Is God unjust? Not at all! 15 For he says to Moses, "I will have mercy on whom I have mercy, and I will have compassion on whom I have compassion." 16 It does not, therefore, depend on man's desire or effort, but on God's mercy. 17 For the Scripture says to Pharaoh: "I raised you up for this very purpose, that I might display my power in you and that my name might be proclaimed in all the earth." 18 Therefore God has mercy on whom he wants to have mercy, and he hardens whom he wants to harden. 19 One of you will say to me: "Then why does God still blame us? For who resists his will?" 20 But who are you, O man, to talk back to God? "Shall what is formed say to him who formed it, 'Why did you make me like this?' " 21 Does not the potter have the right to make out of the same lump of clay some pottery for noble purposes and some for common use? 22 What if God, choosing to show his wrath and make his power known, bore with great patience the objects of his wrath--prepared for destruction? 23 What if he did this to make the riches of his glory known to the objects of his mercy, whom he prepared in advance for glory-- 24 even us, whom he also called, not only from the Jews but also from the Gentiles? 25 As he says in Hosea: "I will call them 'my people' who are not my people; and I will call her 'my loved one' who is not my loved one," 26 and, "It will happen that in the very place where it was said to them, 'You are not my people,' they will be called 'sons of the living God.' " 27 Isaiah cries out concerning Israel: "Though the number of the Israelites be like the sand by the sea, only the remnant will be saved. 28 For the Lord will carry out his sentence on earth with speed and finality." 29 It is just as Isaiah said previously: "Unless the Lord Almighty had left us descendants, we would have become like Sodom, we would have been like Gomorrah. 30 What then shall we say? That the Gentiles, who did not pursue righteousness, have obtained it, a *righteousness that is by faith; **31** but Israel, who pursued a law of righteousness, has not attained it. **32** Why not? Because they pursued it not by faith but as if it were by works. They stumbled over the "stumbling stone." **33** As it is written: "See, I lay in Zion a stone that causes men to stumble and a rock that makes them fall, and the one who trusts in him will never be put to shame."*

J. R. R. Tolkien's *Lord of the Rings* trilogy is actually the story of a very long hike (with a few battles thrown in) to Mordor. Frodo Baggins, a lowly hobbit, is entrusted to carry the ring of power on this hike. Frodo is surrounded by powerful warriors and wizards who make up the Fellowship of the Ring. At one point on the hike, Boromir of Gondor decides that the ring would best be cared for by a mighty warrior such as himself. Those who know the end of the story realize that Boromir is no match for the ring and, if he takes it, will be turned to evil and all will be lost. However, if you don't know the end, Boromir looks like a much better choice to carry the ring than Frodo. Why would Gandalf the wizard choose Frodo over Boromir for such a difficult task? Because he knew the desired end. Who held the ring was not as important as the destiny of the ring, for the destiny of the ring would impact the whole Middle Earth.

At the end of our last chapter, we read that God chose Abraham out of all of the people living in his day. He also chose Isaac over Ishmael and chose Jacob over Esau. We also learned that God's choices were not based on heritage or behavior. God's choices were based on the promise; they were based on what will bring about the desired end that God had in mind. Who was chosen was not as important as God's overall purpose.

---

*Circle the phrases **is God unjust** (14) and **why does God still blame us** (19). Highlight the phrases **in all the earth** (17), **objects of wrath** (22), **objects of mercy** (23), **my people** (25), **my loved one** (25) and **sons of the living God** (26). Draw a square around the word **Gentiles** (30) and draw a line connecting each highlighted phrase to this word.*

God's Choice and God's Plan

Our natural reaction to the series of choices God made is to cry "Foul!" This isn't fair! Well, we are in good company because Paul anticipated the church at Rome would have the same response. He didn't ignore the problem but promptly addressed it (14). His answer only makes sense if we keep it in the context of the end of God's plan. We made note of it in our last chapter. God's plan was for the Gentiles (and Jews) to obtain righteousness by faith (31). It is important to see that throughout this passage, God was not talking about individual people being chosen while others are not. He was talking about the fact that the Gentiles are chosen. The choices that God made under the Old Covenant were all prerequisites to the power of the Gospel bringing in a righteousness by faith to all people! God's desire was that all people would be declared righteous.

When Moses went up on Mt. Sinai to receive the Ten Commandments, he also made a request (which sounded a little like a demand) for God to reveal Himself. God, in His mercy decided to grant that request, but reminded Moses that He had the authority to show mercy and compassion on whomever He willed (Exodus 33:19). He was not showing Moses His glory because Moses asked, but because He chose to be merciful to Moses. Moses' view of God's glory would help Moses be the leader that God needed him to be in order for God's plan to be fulfilled. God's choice is always consistent with His ultimate plan.

Earlier, when Moses appeared before Pharaoh, asking for the release of the Jews, God chose to harden Pharaoh's heart, which brought on the ten plagues. God reminded Moses that He could have wiped Egypt from the face of the earth with one plague, but Pharaoh was to play a part in God's redemptive plan. God was going to use Pharaoh to show the world His mighty power (Exodus 9:16).

These two examples raise another objection. If God was going to harden people's hearts so that they sin, how could those people be held accountable for their sin (19)? To answer this, Paul pulls out some heavy artillery from the Old Testament arsenal. He quoted Isaiah 29:16 and Isaiah 45:9 which portrayed God as the potter and Israel as the clay. These verses were written during a very difficult time in Israel's history. Wrath, judgment, and condemnation were bearing down on them. The people naturally questioned God. God answered through this illustration of potter and clay, essentially saying, "I am God and you are not!"

Of course, Paul is right. God has the authority to make any choice He wants, and we have no right to question Him. However, Paul followed this up by making a suggestion as to why God made these choices. What if (23) while God was showing the world His wrath through Pharaoh, He was also being patient with the objects of wrath prepared for destruction (22). God's ultimate plan included the salvation of the Gentiles (which includes Egypt). At the time of Moses, Israel was enjoying their status as God's chosen ones, and the Gentiles were the objects of wrath, headed for destruction. What God was revealing through Paul was that even then, He had the Gentiles in mind and was working a plan to bring salvation to them as well. His heart was to make them objects of mercy (23), not just Jews but Gentiles as well (24).

Paul immediately followed this up with quotes from the prophet Hosea (1:10, 2:23) that allude to the fact that a group of people who were currently not considered the people of God would become the people of God. This thread of promise to the Gentile world runs through the Old Testament, but the nation of Israel was so focused on their "chosen" status that they could not see it. Isaiah reminded Israel that being a Jew by heritage was not going to save them. In the end, only a remnant would be saved (Isaiah 10:22), because righteousness would not come through bloodline but by faith. In fact, the remnant of Israel was only a result of the mercy of God. If not for His mercy to Israel, they would have become like Sodom and Gomorrah (Isaiah 1:9).

Notice that not once in this passage was an individual mentioned that was chosen to go to Heaven or chosen to go to Hell. This idea of election or predestination that Paul introduced in Romans 9 was not about individuals, it was about Jews and Gentiles. In His sovereignty, God chose Israel to be the recipients of the Old Covenant and gave them the standard of His righteousness, the law. But now under the New Covenant He chose to allow any who would come by faith to partake of His righteousness, including Gentiles.

---

*Circle the phrases **what then shall we say** (30) and **why not** (32). Underline the phrases **righteousness that is by faith** (30), **law of righteousness** (31) and **not by faith** (32).*

Our Choices

In the final verses of this chapter, Paul brought the discussion back to the Gospel that revealed a righteousness that is by faith (1:18). What is the end result of all of God's sovereign choices? What shall we say (30)? The end result was that Gentiles who would have been considered objects of wrath under the Old Covenant had now obtained the status of being right, or enjoying the life that God always intended for them (righteous). They obtained this not by obeying the law but by believing in the sacrifice of Christ on their behalf. The Jews on the other hand, who had been considered the objects of mercy had not found that same righteousness by trying to obey the law. The law, however, was not the problem. The problem was that they had not been able to put their faith in Jesus. Instead of being "the way," He became a "stumbling block" for them (32). The Jews wanted to count on their status as God's Chosen and would not take responsibility to make the choice to receive the sacrifice of Christ personally. It is interesting that Romans 9 is often used to teach a theological system that promotes the idea that God is the only one who chooses, when in the end, Israel does not obtain righteousness because they do not choose it.

Rather than this being a chapter that confuses or even angers us, it is a chapter that causes us to rejoice. If we have put our faith in Jesus, we are no longer objects of wrath (1:18, 8:1). We are objects of His mercy (23), his loved ones (25) and sons of the living God (26). This is good news! This is the Gospel.

Questions to Ponder:

1. What all does God call the Gentiles in this passage? How does this illustrate the Gospel?

2. How do God's choices relate to His plan? Give examples both from the Bible and from your own

3. What choice do WE have in this matter?

Day 25

♦♦♦♦♦♦♦♦♦♦♦♦♦♦♦♦♦♦♦♦♦♦♦

More Good News!
(Romans 10:1-13)

1 Brothers, my heart's desire and prayer to God for the Israelites is that they may be saved. 2 For I can testify about them that they are zealous for God, but their zeal is not based on knowledge. 3 Since they did not know the righteousness that comes from God and sought to establish their own, they did not submit to God's righteousness. 4 Christ is the end of the law so that there may be righteousness for everyone who believes. 5 Moses describes in this way the righteousness that is by the law: "The man who does these things will live by them." 6 But the righteousness that is by faith says: "Do not say in your heart, 'Who will ascend into heaven?' " (that is, to bring Christ down) 7 "or 'Who will descend into the deep?' " (that is, to bring Christ up from the dead). 8 But what does it say? "The word is near you; it is in your mouth and in your heart," that is, the word of faith we are proclaiming: 9 That if you confess with your mouth, "Jesus is Lord," and believe in your heart that God raised him from the dead, you will be saved. 10 For it is with your heart that you believe and are justified, and it is with your mouth that you confess and are saved. 11 As the Scripture says, "Anyone who trusts in him will never be put to shame." 12 For there is no difference between Jew and Gentile--the same Lord is Lord of all and richly blesses all who call on him, 13 for, "Everyone who calls on the name of the Lord will be saved."

Glacier National Park in northern Montana is considered a hiker's paradise. With over 700 miles of trails there is something for everyone to enjoy. One of the most popular trails for the serious hiking enthusiast is the 10-day trek over the Continental Divide right across the backbone of the park. If you like wildlife, hikers report seeing grizzlies, wolves, moose, mountain lions, and mountain goats. If you like variety, there are shear peaks, glaciers, alpine lakes, snowfields, and fields of wildflowers. One hiker described his experience by saying that every day of the hike was better than the day before! (*www.nps.gov/glac*).

Our trek through Romans has taken us more than 10 days, but we can certainly say that each day the truth keeps getting better and better. In Romans 10, Paul begins to compound the good news with even better news.

Underline the phrases **zealous for God** *(2),* **zeal is not based on knowledge** *(2),* **sought to establish their own** *(3) and* **Christ is the end of the law** *(4).*

Good News

You can stop striving to be righteous. This is good news! Imagine yourself seeing an advertisement on television for a brand new IS 350 F Sport Lexus. Immediately you fall in love! You drive right to the Lexus dealer to pick up your new car. Unfortunately, the salesman says that financially you do not qualify for the price tag of $43,999. In your mind, you immediately begin to think of ways you can scrape together more money, but as you work, the salesman interrupts you to let you know he has decided to give you the car for free. This is good news!

That is exactly how Paul began Romans 10. He again expressed his desire for Israel's salvation (1). He even bragged about the energy and effort that they put into following after God. The problem was that they were trying to establish their own righteousness (3) according to the law. The law has over 600 specific commands to be obeyed (on top of the BIG 10). No one could consistently keep all of these commands; no one could attain to this standard of righteousness. So, they came up short (3:23). Their efforts were commendable, but they were based on faulty information. The law was no longer applicable because Christ is the end of the law. Righteousness was no longer to be worked toward on the basis of the law, it was to be given freely through Christ who did fulfill the law completely! So while Paul began with bad news (your striving brings you up short) he ended with good news (righteousness is not earned, it's given!).

> *Draw a square around the phrases* **Moses describes** *(5) and the* **righteousness that is by faith says** *(6).*

More Good News

There is more good news. Not only do we not have to exhaust ourselves trying to be righteous, we also don't have to worry about how others evaluate us. Those who put themselves under the law of Moses will be evaluated by how they obey, the way they live their lives on an everyday basis (5). That would be scary! Out of 365 days this year, I'm not sure I would get a good score. When we receive the righteousness that is by faith, we no longer try to say who is going to Heaven (6) or who is going to Hell (7) based on their behavior. If behavior were the chief indicator of righteousness, we wouldn't need Jesus at all. While Jesus did say, *By their fruits you shall know them* (Matthew 7:20), it is not the criteria by which God will make the final judgment. Our faith is the catalyst for salvation, not our works (Ephesians 2:8,9). While we might be tempted to look around and determine that certain people are going to Hell and others are not, God knows their hearts. In Christ we have been evaluated and found acceptable.

> *Highlight the phrases* **submit to God's righteousness** *(3),* **confess** *(9),* **believe** *(9) and* **calls on** *(13).*

Even More Good News

Guess what? More good news! Because all of our striving could never attain to God's righteous standard, God did it for us. Christ became the end of the law by doing what we could not and then dying to exchange His righteousness for our sin, thus completely paying our penalty and awarding us His righteousness. There is no striving, there is only choosing. Just as in the Garden of Eden, man used his free will to choose a path to life apart from God (independence), now man must choose to find life only through

God (dependence). By eating of the fruit of the tree of knowledge of good and evil, man declared that he could make life work on his own. He could be right or be all that he was created to be without God. Now, having come to the end of ourselves, we must choose the opposite. We must stop striving to attain our own righteousness and submit to His righteousness (3). We must bow the knee to Him and admit that our own efforts are worthless. We must agree with God (confess) that Jesus is the only Righteous One and put our faith (believe) with our heart that His resurrection can bring us new life. You may look at the "we musts" in the past few sentences and think that we are having to work for our righteousness. The truth is that we are not really doing anything, we are simply responding to something that has already been done. Everything that was needed to accomplish our salvation (deliverance from wrath) has been accomplished by God through the death, burial, and resurrection of Jesus. Now, we must choose. Choosing involves submission, confession, faith, and connection. We call on His name. We connect with His Person. We choose. While many use Romans 9 and 10 to teach that we don't choose at all, because God chooses us, the Scriptures could not be more clear. *We* submit, *we* confess, *we* believe, and *we* call on.

---

*Circle the phrases **everyone who believes (4), anyone who trusts in him (11), all who call upon him (12)** and **everyone** (13).*

The Best News

Having circled the phrases indicated above we can clearly see that this Gospel is for everyone! This is the best news! He even makes sure to say that there is no difference between Jew and Gentile (12). The Jews were God's chosen people throughout the Old Testament. But we have seen in Romans 9 that the Gentiles were always meant to be recipients of God's righteousness as well. He chose them too! The Jews were chosen to prepare the way, give us the law, and give us Christ, but all are chosen to receive this righteousness by faith (1:18). This is not teaching universalism. There is still choice involved. The phrases we circled include a response on our part to make the promise effective.

Not only is salvation offered to everyone, but once received, it is 100% guaranteed. Paul says that *anyone who trusts in him will never be put to shame* (11). The word used for shame here literally means dishonored or disappointed. The Gospel never dishonors or disappoints us. We can count on the promise of God which says that by faith we become right, we get the life we were always meant to live, we can live abundantly (John 10:10). Certainly we may go through difficult times, but in the end, the Gospel will not disappoint us. Remember our previous reference to the movie, *The Best Exotic Marigold Hotel*? The hotel owner, Sonny, tries to help the residents deal with their disappointments in their accommodations. He tells them, "It will all be okay in the end, so if it is not okay, it is not the end!" I like to tell myself that in the middle of a bad day. The Gospel is guaranteed, it will not disappoint! It really will be okay in the end... guaranteed.

Questions to Ponder:
1. Make a list of the good news shared in this passage.

2. Make a list of choices we must make mentioned in this passage.

Day 26

◆◆◆◆◆◆◆◆◆◆◆◆◆◆◆◆◆◆◆◆◆◆◆◆

What About Them?
(Romans 10:14-21)

14 How, then, can they call on the one they have not believed in? And how can they believe in the one of whom they have not heard? And how can they hear without someone preaching to them? 15 And how can they preach unless they are sent? As it is written, "How beautiful are the feet of those who bring good news!" 16 But not all the Israelites accepted the good news. For Isaiah says, "Lord, who has believed our message?" 17 Consequently, faith comes from hearing the message, and the message is heard through the word of Christ. 18 But I ask: Did they not hear? Of course they did: "Their voice has gone out into all the earth, their words to the ends of the world." 19 Again I ask: Did Israel not understand? First, Moses says, "I will make you envious by those who are not a nation; I will make you angry by a nation that has no understanding." 20 And Isaiah boldly says, "I was found by those who did not seek me; I revealed myself to those who did not ask for me." 21 But concerning Israel he says, "All day long I have held out my hands to a disobedient and obstinate people."

The Appalachian Trail is a 2200-mile long hiking trail that extends from Maine to Georgia in the Eastern United States. The trail is a favorite for hikers from all over the world. Some parts of the trail are more difficult than others and those who maintain the trail do their best to inform hikers of the dangers. Just before entering what is known as the 100-mile wilderness area of the trail in Maine, hikers will read the following warning sign:

There are no places to obtain supplies or get help until Abol Bridge 100 miles North. Do not attempt this section unless you have a minimum of 10 days of supplies and are fully equipped. This is the longest wilderness section of the entire Appalachian Trail and its difficulty should not be underestimated. Good hiking!

150

This sign has saved many lives. However, in spite of the sign there have been those who have entered this area unprepared and have either lost their lives or had to be rescued because of injury or lack of supplies. With such a clear warning, how can this be? If you stay on the trail, it would be impossible to miss the sign which is large and in a prominent location. However, some chose to walk right past the sign and never even read it. Others who read it didn't understand it because they hadn't learned English well enough. Still others read it, understoodd it but didn't believe its message. They scoffed that the trail guides were exaggerating, that they would be fine and that this sign was written for beginners. Regardless of the reason, it is dangerous not to heed this important warning and you can read many blogs about hikers who paid the price for ignoring it.

In Romans 10, the Apostle Paul has just emphatically stated that whoever calls on the Lord's name will receive salvation (13). He even emphasized that there is no distinction between Jews and Gentiles in regard to this call (12) and that this faith decision is not far out of our reach but it is near to us all (8). So how is it that there are still so many people who do not believe? This is the subject Paul intends to cover in the last part of Romans 10.

> *Circle the words **call on** (14), **believed in** (14), **heard** (14), **someone preaching** (14), and **sent** (15). Underline the words **message** (17) and **word of Christ** (17) and draw a line from the word **heard** (14) to both of these words. Underline the world **faith** (17) and draw a line connecting it with the words **believed in** (14).*

Call on the Lord

If we look at all of the words we have circled in these verses we will see that there is a progression that leads to the moment when we *call on* the name of the Lord for salvation. The progression begins when someone is sent with the message. Paul identified himself to the Romans as an apostle (1:1). The word apostle literally means "one who is sent". The disciples of Christ became the apostles of Christ after He gave them the Great Commission, telling them to *go into all the world and preach the gospel* (Mark 16:15). God does the sending and we are responsible for the going. Let's not fall into the trap of believing that only some are chosen as apostles. We are all apostles or ambassadors for Christ (II Corinthians 5:20). Neither let us fall into the trap of believing that God has already chosen who will be saved. Those who interpret Romans 9 and 10 to teach the doctrine of election and predestination would have to completely ignore this part of the chapter. A messenger would not be needed if those who were chosen would all believe anyway! So, fellow messengers, how are we doing with sharing the message?

The progression continues with hearing. The messenger cannot be effective if those he is sent to do not hear the message. Now there is a difference between hearing and *hearing*. Sometimes I hear what my wife is saying but I don't really hear her, in other words I don't look deeper than the words to her heart or the need she may be expressing. In order to call on the name of the Lord for salvation people must really hear the message. What is the message? The message is the gospel, the gospel that Paul has been talking about throughout Romans beginning at 1:18. Jesus Christ, died, was buried and rose again to make us righteous and give us life. The message is the good news about Christ. The message is not *God loves you*, or *do unto others as they do unto you* or *be good*! The message is Christ! The gospel is Christ! And it is good news. Paul quotes Isaiah in saying that the news of the gospel is so good that it makes the feet of the messenger appear beautiful to those who hear. (15; Isaiah 52:7). That would be miraculous for me because my feet are dry, scaly with browned toenails... and they smell! The proclamation of this message is called preaching (14). Somehow in our culture the preacher has become a paid position whose responsibility is to speak *thus saith the Lord* every week for no more than 35 minutes! But the word *preacher* literally means one who heralds or publically proclaims a message. If we are all apostles, then we are all preachers, called by God to herald the gospel to those we meet and know.

Hearing the message though is not enough. Before someone is willing to call on the name of the Lord for salvation, they must believe (14). Faith is the choice that each of us must make in order to be saved. God has done all of the work of salvation, we do not need to strive or try hard to be good, we simply choose. Actually when God put Adam and Eve in the garden, He wanted them to have faith in Him that He could give them life. When they chose the other tree, they were not acting in faith and whatever is not of faith is sin (Romans 14:23). This is the point at which the responsibility of the messenger ends. We go and we proclaim the gospel in a way that people can hear and understand it but we cannot make another person choose. Paul said that this righteousness is available by faith (1:18) and faith is the responsibility of each person. Faith in the finished work of Christ leads to a desire to call on the Lord for salvation. We have already seen that this calling involves both the heart and the mouth (10) and that those who call on Him will never be disappointed (11).

Put a box around the phrases **did they not hear** *(18) and* **did Israel not understand** *(19).*

What About Those Who Have Never Heard?

The delineation of this progression toward salvation brings up a question. It is a question that the Romans had in their day and a question that is still asked today. What about those who have never heard? Paul actually asks the question a little differently, *did they all hear* (18)? Paul's answer to the question is a little confusing. He answers *of course they did* (18). In defense of his answer he quotes from Psalm 19. This Psalm of David does relate to the topic of people knowing:

1 The heavens declare the glory of God; the skies proclaim the work of his hands. 2 Day after day they pour forth speech; night after night they display knowledge. 3 There is no speech or language where their voice is not heard. 4 Their voice goes out into all the earth, their words to the ends of the world.

Paul's point here is that God has made Himself known to the world through His creation which points toward the Creator 24/7. While this point is well taken, for most it does not answer the overall problem. If it is the word of Christ that must be heard, how does seeing God in creation help us with that? God is faithful and gives light and knowledge to those who seek Him. If a people respond in faith to God because of what is revealed to them (i.e. creation) then He is faithful to those who seek after Him to give them the opportunity to hear more (Gospel).

Another possible explanation hinges on the way Paul asks the question in 10:18, **did** they not hear? It is possible that in the past, when the world was less populated, all nations heard the message of the gospel or that through those who believed it was possible for the message to make it to the whole world. It became then, the responsibility of those who heard to proclaim the message throughout their region and to the next generation. If your great grandfather was a strong Christian but you grew up never hearing the gospel, is that God's fault or is it the fault of those who knew the message and did not share it? Jesus was very clear when He gave the great Commission that it was the role of the disciples (learners of Christ) to be the apostles (messengers of Christ).

But in the context of Paul's discussion throughout Romans, the larger question concerns the Jews. They had been told to obey the law, offer the sacrifices, confess to the priest and they would be God's people. How could God keep them in the dark about this message of the gospel and the inclusion of the Gentiles? Did they truly not understand? It is hard to believe that Israel did not know. When God initially came to Abraham to found the nation of Israel, He told Abraham that he would be the father of many nations. Now Israel was a great nation but it wasn't many nations! Obviously God's promise through Abraham was always meant to impact more than Israel. Paul quotes Moses and Isaiah to show that Israel was told all through the Old Testament about the coming of the gospel and the inclusion of the Gentiles. Moses had sung a song to Israel In Deuteronomy 32 in which he told them that because of their idolatry, God would make Israel envy by using a nation who had no understanding of the Old Covenant (19; Deuteronomy 32:21). He quotes Isaiah who prophesied 600 years before Christ that God would reveal Himself to those who were not seeking Him and that God found Israel to be both disobedient and obstinate (20-21; Isaiah 65:1,2).

So concerning the availability of the message of the Gospel, Paul's conclusion is the same as what he taught about mankind's excuse in Romans 1, *men are without excuse* (1:20). The witness of God in creation, the message of the whole Old Testament and the responsibility of believers to share the gospel all combined make worldwide proclamation of the gospel possible.

So fellow hikers, the sign is clearly visible on the trail and the instructions are easy to understand. So how have so many missed it? Some, having rejected the witness of creation are not on the trail of pursuing God so they did not see the sign. Others have not been taught to read the sign by those who were called to teach them. Others do not see their need to obey the message. Have you read the sign and obeyed? Are you sharing this important message with those who follow you on the trail?

Questions to Ponder:

1. Do you agree that God's warning about the gospel is as clear as the sign on the Appalachian Trail? Why or why not?

2. Write out the profession that leads to salvation explained in these verses.

3. Do you agree with the conclusion that "all are without excuse"? Why or why not?

Day 27

◆◆◆◆◆◆◆◆◆◆◆◆◆◆◆◆◆◆◆◆◆◆◆◆

Whose Fault Is It?
(Romans 11:1-10)

1 I ask then: Did God reject his people? By no means! I am an Israelite myself, a descendant of Abraham, from the tribe of Benjamin. 2 God did not reject his people, whom he foreknew. Don't you know what the Scripture says in the passage about Elijah--how he appealed to God against Israel: 3 "Lord, they have killed your prophets and torn down your altars; I am the only one left, and they are trying to kill me" ? 4 And what was God's answer to him? "I have reserved for myself seven thousand who have not bowed the knee to Baal." 5 So too, at the present time there is a remnant chosen by grace. 6 And if by grace, then it is no longer by works; if it were, grace would no longer be grace. 7 What then? What Israel sought so earnestly it did not obtain, but the elect did. The others were hardened, 8 as it is written: "God gave them a spirit of stupor, eyes so that they could not see and ears so that they could not hear, to this very day." 9 And David says: "May their table become a snare and a trap, a stumbling block and a retribution for them. 10 May their eyes be darkened so they cannot see, and their backs be bent forever."

Each year 1-2 hikers lose their lives on the slopes of Mt. Ranier in Washington State. The mountain rises over 14,000 feet and is covered with snow and ice at the summit year round. Glaciers and ice fields make hiking treacherous and storms can sweep in quickly dumping several feet of snow, even in the summer! Warnings, instructions and recommendations for safety precautions are widely publicized to anyone attempting to make the climb. Most who perish were ill-equipped or failed to heed the warnings. This fact does not stop the families of those who perished from filing lawsuits against the National Park service. Somehow faulty human logic concludes that if something bad happened to someone in a National Park, it must be the Park's fault.

---

*Draw a square around the phrase **Did God reject his people** (1)
and around the word **no** (1). Underline the phrase **I am an
Israelite** (1), **there is a remnant** (5) and **others were hardened**
(7). Number these three phrases 1, 2 and 3.*

Did God Reject Israel?

In Romans 10 Paul communicated his desire for the nation of
Israel. He passionately desired for them to receive the
righteousness that is by faith. He sadly reports, however, that
Israel continued to try to establish their own righteousness through
the law and so still needed to be saved (10:1-3). This brings up a
question that Paul uses to open Romans 11; Did God reject his
people (1)? The word reject here is a harsh one, literally meaning
to shove away. Like our hikers, human logic says if Israel's status
with God has changed, it must be God's fault!

The short answer to Paul's question is no (1), God is not rejecting
Israel. He goes on to offer three proofs. The first is Paul Himself.
Paul is a Jew, a descendant of Abraham, a member of the tribe of
Benjamin and Paul has received the righteousness by faith. He is
an Israelite and he has not been rejected.

The second proof is a reminder of the difference between God's
perspective and man's perspective. Here Paul uses the example of
Elijah and the prophets of Baal. God had instructed the prophet
Elijah to go to Ahab, King of Israel and tell him that it would not
rain for 3 years. This drought was meant as a judgment because
King Ahab promoted idolatry (I Kings 17:1-2). Elijah then had to
hide from Ahab's wrath. While hiding by the brook Cherith God
cared for him with water from the brook and food which was
brought to him by ravens (I Kings 17:6). When the brook dried up
Elijah moved to the home of the widow of Zarephath who took
care of him until the time that God called him to go present himself
again to King Ahab. The meeting took place on Mount Carmel
between Elijah, prophet of God and 450 prophets of Baal. The
contest was simple. Both would build an altar and the first god to

send fire to the altar would be the true God. Of course, God won and Elijah killed all 450 prophets of Baal, what a victory! However, Ahab's wife, Jezebel was quite upset at the outcome and she ordered the death of Elijah. Now Elijah runs for his life, becomes suicidal and complains to God that he is the *only prophet left in Israel*. I'm sure after all Elijah went through he felt like the only one left and he felt like God was asking too much of him. God reminded Elijah that he was not alone. God still had a remnant of believers in Israel, 7000 to be exact. It looked like God had abandoned His people, it felt like God had abandoned His people but God had NOT abandoned His people! Paul reminds the Roman church that in spite of Israel's overall rejection of God's righteousness by faith and in spite of the fact that it looks like God has rejected His people, God still has a remnant of Israelites who have abandoned their system of works and accepted God's grace.

It doesn't seem fair that what Israel worked so hard to achieve, they did not obtain (7) but that it was given to the elect (Gentiles) by grace. How could this happen? The answer to this is Paul's third proof. He says Israel (except for the remnant) was hardened. This word for hardened literally means *to cover with a thick skin like a callous, to become insensitive*. In other words, Israel had focused so much on their privileged position under the law, they became insensitive to the message of grace. After decades of going through the religious rituals, their hearts became hardened to God's voice. By the time Jesus came they didn't even recognize God when He lived among them. This hardening could very well have been more than a learned insensitivity, it could also include a judicial act of God. Just as we learned in Romans 1, God could have "given them over" to their own thought processes because of their rejection and idolatry. In Romans 1, mankind refused to acknowledge God so their hearts were darkened (1:21). If the people of Israel are no longer considered the people of God because they failed to heed God's warnings and instructions, is it because God rejected them or because they rejected God? This is the point Paul is making: God did NOT reject His people, His people rejected Him.

> *Circle the words **Elijah (2)**, **God's answer (4)**, **it is written (8)** and **David says (9)**.*

Did Israel Reject God?

The Jewish people were so proud of their heritage and their relationship with Jehovah under the law that it seemed inconceivable to them that Israel would reject God. This is why they assumed God had rejected them! But Paul is a student of the Old Testament and in this passage he masterfully reveals that Israel's rejection of God is not something new or unexpected. He begins with the prophet Elijah. As far as prophets go, Elijah was at the top of the list. Elijah was to return before the coming of the Messiah. Elijah appeared with Moses on the mount of Transfiguration. Paul did not randomly choose to use the story of Elijah. The bottom line of this story is that, in the days when King Ahab and Queen Jezebel ruled over Israel, only a remnant of Israel still followed Jehovah, the rest of Israel had utterly rejected God in favor of idols. Paul quotes Elijah and God from I Kings 19 showing the extent of Israel's rejection of God.

The hardening of Israel's heart is also not something new. The spirit of stupor that Paul talks about (9) is a quotation both from Moses (Deuteronomy 29:4) and the prophet Isaiah (Isaiah 29:10). Throughout Israel's history, God's people hardened their hearts against the message and plan of God. Finally, Paul brings out the big guns... David, King David, the man after God's own heart, the originator of the Kingly line that would usher in the Messiah. David prophesied in Psalm 69:22-23 that Israel would stumble over God's goodness to them (the table set before them) and that they would be bent low under the burden of the law that could never set them free.

In spite of all of this, God is not finished with Israel. There is still a remnant and God will be glorified through that remnant. Even when it seems God is finished with us, He shows that He is ever faithful. God does not reject His people and He even offers them salvation after they have rejected Him. Grace!

Questions to Ponder

1. Are you blaming God for something in your life that may be your own fault? Or the fault of someone else?

2. Read the story of Elijah in I Kings 17-19. Have you ever felt like Elijah? Does God's reassurance to Elijah encourage you (I Kings 19:5-18)?

3. How have you experienced "hardening" in your own life or seen it in the lives of others?

Day 28

◆◆◆◆◆◆◆◆◆◆◆◆◆◆◆◆◆◆◆◆◆◆◆◆

Can Israel Recover?
(Romans 11:11-24)

11 Again I ask: Did they stumble so as to fall beyond recovery? Not at all! Rather, because of their transgression, salvation has come to the Gentiles to make Israel envious. 12 But if their transgression means riches for the world, and their loss means riches for the Gentiles, how much greater riches will their fullness bring! 13 I am talking to you Gentiles. Inasmuch as I am the apostle to the Gentiles, I make much of my ministry 14 in the hope that I may somehow arouse my own people to envy and save some of them. 15 For if their rejection is the reconciliation of the world, what will their acceptance be but life from the dead? 16 If the part of the dough offered as firstfruits is holy, then the whole batch is holy; if the root is holy, so are the branches. 17 If some of the branches have been broken off, and you, though a wild olive shoot, have been grafted in among the others and now share in the nourishing sap from the olive root, 18 do not boast over those branches. If you do, consider this: You do not support the root, but the root supports you. 19 You will say then, "Branches were broken off so that I could be grafted in." 20 Granted. But they were broken off because of unbelief, and you stand by faith. Do not be arrogant, but be afraid. 21 For if God did not spare the natural branches, he will not spare you either. 22 Consider therefore the kindness and sternness of God: sternness to those who fell, but kindness to you, provided that you continue in his kindness. Otherwise, you also will be cut off. 23 And if they do not persist in unbelief, they will be grafted in, for God is able to graft them in again. 24 After all, if you were cut out of an olive tree that is wild by nature, and contrary to nature were grafted into a cultivated olive tree, how much more readily will these, the natural branches, be grafted into their own olive tree!

While hiking the trails, we may run across many different types of trees. Imagine coming upon an apple tree in the woods. Half of the tree is filled with beautiful white apple blossoms and the other side seems barren. Our first conclusion is half of the tree has succumbed to some disease and is dead. Upon closer examination, we find that the barren side has short stalks from which blossoms have already fallen to the ground. A later blossoming-type of apple tree has been grafted in to the original tree so that half of the tree blooms early while the other half blooms late. Same tree, same roots, different branches. In Romans 11, Paul used this analogy of grafting in branches to describe the relationship between the Jews and the Gentiles.

---

*Draw a box around the question **Did they stumble as to fall beyond recovery** and the answer **not at all** (11). Underline the phrases **because of their transgression salvation has come to the Gentiles** (11), **arouse my own people to envy** (14), their **acceptance be but life from the dead** (15) and **firstfruits is holy, then the whole batch is holy** (16). Number these four statements 1-4.*

Positives From a Negative

Paul is continuing the discussion he began about the Jewish people in 11:1. In the first part of this chapter he answered the question "Did God reject Israel?" But he changed the question a little to "Has Israel fallen so far, they cannot recover?" The answer to both questions is no.

Even though Israel's rejection of God looked like a negative, Paul listed four positive things that could flow out of their rejection. First, salvation by faith, which was rejected by the Jews, was then offered to the Gentiles, resulting in the salvation of multitudes of people. Paul was commissioned by God as an apostle to the Gentiles (Acts 9:15), but in every town that Paul visited, he took the Gospel to the Jews first. Only after the Jews rejected his message did he turn to the Gentiles. In Acts 13 while ministering in Pisidian Antioch, Paul said to the Jews of that city, *"We had to speak the word of God to you first. Since you reject it and do not consider yourselves worthy of eternal life, we now turn to the Gentiles"* (42).

Second, Paul said that multitudes of Gentiles coming to faith actually made the Jewish people envious. Seeing the type of relationship with God that comes through Christ including rest from striving for righteousness by the law, would cause some Jews to look into this new faith and be saved (14). I wonder if this is true today? Do people who see our relationship with God become envious and want to learn more about Christ? If we are living in the freedom and rest of grace, experiencing life in relationship with God as a righteous son or daughter, I believe it will make others envious. But if we continue to strive to please God, believing that we must constantly try to live up to the law, we will turn others off from the gospel.

Third, Paul wondered out loud what impact Israel's salvation would have on the world. If their rejection of the Gospel brought about life (through the salvation of the Gentiles) their acceptance of the Gospel would likely bring about resurrection. This phrase reminds me of Ezekiel's vision of the Valley of Dry Bones in Ezekiel 37. In the vision, the prophet saw some old dry dead bones (representing Israel) join together and come back to life. The prophet prophesied that once that happened God declared, *"My dwelling place will be with them; I will be their God, and they will be my people."* Truly Israel has not fallen too far to be restored, even if they currently resemble dry bones.

Finally, Paul used an example from the Old Testament sacrificial system. In the sacrifices made at the beginning of the harvest (first fruits), a loaf of bread was made from the grain. A piece of the loaf was offered to God as a firstfruits offering. The idea was that if the firstfruit **part** of the loaf was holy, the **whole** loaf was holy. Paul may have been referring to Abraham as the firstfruits of Israel. Abraham believed God and was declared righteous (Romans 4:3). The possibility of the whole loaf (Israel) being righteous does exist.

So, in spite of their idolatry, in spite of their rejection of Christ, and in spite of their unbelief, God is still extending grace toward Israel.

---

*Circle the phrase **branches have been broken off** (17), **wild olive shoot** (17) and **olive root** (17). Highlight the words **unbelief** and **by faith** (20) and the words **kindness and sternness of God** (22).*

No Bragging Rights

Next, Paul used the analogy of the olive tree. In this analogy, the olive tree is the Kingdom of God. The root of the olive tree is God Himself; the branches broken off represent Israel; and the wild olive shoot grafted in represents the Gentiles. God has always been growing His Kingdom. The natural or first branches produced were the Jewish people, called by God through Abraham into a special relationship with Him. These branches were broken off of the tree, removed from the Kingdom because of unbelief. In their place, the Gentiles have been grafted into the Kingdom. This breaking off and grafting in doesn't have anything to do with whether a person is a Jew or Gentile. The Jewish branches were broken off because of unbelief (20) and the Gentile branches were grafted in by faith (20). This summarizes the whole teaching of Romans so far. In order to be a part of God's Kingdom, we must be righteous. The Jews were striving to obey God's righteous law in order to become righteous enough, but true righteousness only comes by faith in Jesus Christ and His righteousness (the Gospel).

The Gentiles should not brag about their new status as branches because they did not accomplish this on their own; it was a gift from God. God's kindness (grace) and sternness (judgment) apply to all. Paul warned us in Romans 1 that the wrath of God was being revealed from Heaven against godlessness. If Gentiles do not believe, they will be cut off as well. It also stands to reason that if the Jews choose to believe, they will be quickly grafted back into the tree as natural branches! Paul was not talking about losing our salvation, he was talking about nations being cut off from salvation because of unbelief or included because of their belief. There is no guarantee that Gentiles will be saved just because they are Gentiles, faith is required.

We need to see that this whole reality hinges on belief. Faith in Christ brings righteousness. It is not our heritage, it is not our performance, and it is not our adherence to any rules or regulations. The branches abide in the tree, nourished by the root in order to produce fruit for the glory of God (John 15). So how does it feel to be a branch on God's olive tree? Righteous!

Questions to Ponder:

1. Write out the four positives that flow out of Israel's rejection of the gospel (in your own words).

2. Draw the olive tree illustration and label it using the information from this passage.

3. What role does belief play in our salvation?

Day 29

◆◆◆◆◆◆◆◆◆◆◆◆◆◆◆◆◆◆◆◆◆◆◆◆◆

Rest and Recap
(Romans 11:25-36)

25 I do not want you to be ignorant of this mystery, brothers, so that you may not be conceited: Israel has experienced a hardening in part until the full number of the Gentiles has come in. 26 And so all Israel will be saved, as it is written: "The deliverer will come from Zion; he will turn godlessness away from Jacob. 27 And this is my covenant with them when I take away their sins." 28 As far as the gospel is concerned, they are enemies on your account; but as far as election is concerned, they are loved on account of the patriarchs, 29 for God's gifts and his call are irrevocable. 30 Just as you who were at one time disobedient to God have now received mercy as a result of their disobedience, 31 so they too have now become disobedient in order that they too may now receive mercy as a result of God's mercy to you. 32 For God has bound all men over to disobedience so that he may have mercy on them all. 33 Oh, the depth of the riches of the wisdom and knowledge of God! How unsearchable his judgments, and his paths beyond tracing out! 34 "Who has known the mind of the Lord? Or who has been his counselor?" 35 "Who has ever given to God, that God should repay him?" 36 For from him and through him and to him are all things. To him be the glory forever!

As we previously mentioned, the Appalachian Trail cuts through 14 different states and is over 2,000 miles long. There are over 250 primitive shelters or lean-to's built at strategic intervals along the trail. Experienced hikers know the advantage of taking regular breaks, having a dry place to sleep, and finding a place to gather with other hikers to exchange stories. It is not surprising that some of the most often-used shelters are found near the most challenging parts of the trail.

On our trek through Romans, we are just finishing up a rather long and difficult section. Paul convinced us that we are all under the wrath of God (1-2), there is a righteousness that comes by faith available to all (3-4), the law could never make us righteous (5-8) and Israel's role in God's plan. In the first parts of chapter 11, He has answered two questions in reference to Israel; 1) Did God reject His people? (11:1), and 2) Did they stumble so as to fall beyond recovery? (11:11). He answers both questions with an emphatic, NO! The remainder of chapter 11 is like a little rest area designed to help us summarize, catch our breath, and prepare to move on to a new topic in Romans 12.

The Summary

Paul didn't introduce any new material into the discussion in these verses, but he did use eight summary statements to drive home his teaching about Israel so as to leave no question in the reader's mind about God's chosen people.

---

*Circle the words **mystery and hardening** (25) and connect them with a line. Place a number one beside these words. Circle the phrase **Israel will be saved** and number it 2. Circle the words **enemies** and **loved** (28) and connect them with a line, numbering them 3. Circle the phrase **God's gifts and call are irrevocable** and number it 4. Circle **God's mercy** (31) and number it 5. Circle the phrase **his paths beyond tracing** out (33) and number it 6. Circle the phrase **who has ever given to God** and number it 7. Circle the phrase **to him be the glory** and number it 8.*

Paul has already explained to the Romans that the Gospel was given first to the Jews, but in pride they rejected it. Some part of their rejection was a judicial act on the part of God to harden their hearts to this message of love and salvation. The result of the Jewish rejection of the Gospel was the offer of salvation to the Gentiles. This was a mystery, not in the sense that it was hard to understand, but in the sense that Israel did not see it coming. The mystery was the hardening of Israel's heart that resulted in the salvation of the Gentiles.

Remembering the two questions Paul had already answered in Romans 11 (1 & 11) regarding Israel, it is important to state emphatically here that after the Gentiles had received the Gospel, the nation of Israel would eventually turn to the Savior. Paul was not speaking in absolute terms here. Just as not ALL of Israel was hardened, not ALL of Israel will be saved. The Old Testament did prophesy a returning of Israel to God through the Gospel (Isaiah 59:20,21; Jeremiah 31:33,34), and Paul felt it important to quote these in his summary.

Since the church at Rome was made up of predominately Gentiles, but also had some Jewish converts, Paul acknowledged the ambivalent feeling toward the Jewish people as a nation. In the first century, before Rome stepped up its persecution of Christians, the Jewish leaders were the number one persecutors of the church. Paul acknowledged this fact but balanced it out with the truth that God loves Israel because of the Patriarchs (Abraham, Isaac, Jacob, etc.,). How does this apply to us today? If only the church at large could be more comfortable with ambivalent feelings toward different groups of people (homosexuals, drug addicts, liturgists, charismatics, etc.,) we would be able to enjoy unity in the Spirit!

Not one to miss a good preaching point, Paul used God's faithfulness to Israel as an opportunity to state that when God gives a gift or a calling, He does not revoke it! Again, the church loves to disqualify people from using their gift or following their calling based upon some behavior pattern or character flaw. I love the word irrevocable... it is so... absolute! David was called to be a King, made bad choices, suffered consequences but continued his calling as a King and died a King. God's calling and gifts are not dependent on our behavior but on His faithfulness and He is faithful.

Grace is one of the words that we mentioned in the introduction that we would be seeing frequently on this journey. This righteousness that comes by faith was going to be a gift, free of charge... grace! Paul used the word mercy here instead of grace, but the concept is the same. Mercy has come full circle. The

Gentiles were considered unclean, outside of the covenant and disobedient but, they have received mercy. The Jews became disobedient when they rejected the Gospel and so now they also receive the same mercy. It is, by the way, the only way we receive God's salvation, by grace.

The Benediction

Paul closed this section out with a beautiful benediction (33-36). Even though, he had tried to answer all of the anticipated questions and objections of the Christians at Rome, he clearly states that God's wisdom is beyond our ability to completely understand. The paths that led to the Gospel, salvation of the Gentiles, ultimate salvation of the Jews, etc., are not paths that we can logically trace because God's thinking is beyond ours. There is a fairly modern Christian song that says "when you can't trace His hand, trust His heart."

Whenever the discussion of election, predestination, God's chosen people, etc., comes up, the word "unfair" is never far from people's lips. We love to look at what God does in His sovereign plan and cry "foul," "unfair!" Paul answered this objection by pointing out that God is the giver (35) of all things. Nothing we have came from any other source, and we have absolutely nothing to give back to Him. The truth is that "unfair" always works out for our good. We get better than we earn!

So how could Paul wrap it all up and say it's not about us, it's about Him. What if he said, *"For from him and through him and to him are all things. To Him be glory forever! Amen!"* I think that will do it!

Questions to Ponder:

1. Can you identify the eight summary statements in this
        passage? List them.

2. It is hard not to have some negative feelings toward people who oppose the truth. How does this passage help us balance out those feelings?

3. Recount some of the ways you have experienced God's unsearchable wisdom?

Day 30

◆◆◆◆◆◆◆◆◆◆◆◆◆◆◆◆◆◆◆◆◆◆◆

What About Behavior?
(Romans 12:1-8)

1 Therefore, I urge you, brothers, in view of God's mercy, to offer your bodies as living sacrifices, holy and pleasing to God--this is your spiritual act of worship. 2 Do not conform any longer to the pattern of this world, but be transformed by the renewing of your mind. Then you will be able to test and approve what God's will is--his good, pleasing and perfect will. 3 For by the grace given me I say to every one of you: Do not think of yourself more highly than you ought, but rather think of yourself with sober judgment, in accordance with the measure of faith God has given you. 4 Just as each of us has one body with many members, and these members do not all have the same function, 5 so in Christ we who are many form one body, and each member belongs to all the others. 6 We have different gifts, according to the grace given us. If a man's gift is prophesying, let him use it in proportion to his faith. 7 If it is serving, let him serve; if it is teaching, let him teach; 8 if it is encouraging, let him encourage; if it is contributing to the needs of others, let him give generously; if it is leadership, let him govern diligently; if it is showing mercy, let him do it cheerfully.

Some of the best short trails I have hiked have been one-way trails. There is a short hike on the Skyline Drive outside of Luray, VA, that leads to a wonderful overlook. The hike is about one mile each way, but is the exact same trail coming down as it is going up. Usually this hike is done without a guide, but one time I was with a group and we had a guide. The guide shared one perspective of the trail going up and then switched to a totally different perspective coming down. It was almost like we were on a different trail even though it was the same scenery.

The Apostle Paul did the same thing as he led us through the book of Romans. In the first 11 chapters, he took us up the trail from a theological perspective. He has explained that we all have a problem (sin and death) and that the problem cannot be resolved by obedience to law (striving) but by receiving the gospel (grace). He explained that it wasn't outward righteousness that gave us life (religion), but the righteousness that comes by faith (relationship through Christ). Now we are turning around to learn how these theological truths translate into our everyday lives. Paul was not discounting the role of obedience and behavior in our lives, but He was saying that changes in behavior must be approached from the proper foundation.

---

*Highlight the word **therefore** (1) and draw an area pointing backwards. Write Chapters 1-11 above the arrow. Highlight **in view of God's mercy** and draw an arrow from that phrase to the word offer (1). Circle the phrase **offer your bodies** (1) and the underline the words/phrases **living sacrifices, holy, pleasing, act of worship** and number them 1 through 4.*

The Big Therefore

Paul used the word "therefore" 21 times in the book of Romans, but we would probably label this use (12:1), the "BIG therefore." Paul seemed to be drawing some conclusions from his entire argument so far found in Romans 1-11. Two things point to this conclusion. The first is that for the first time, Paul was actually urging the Roman Christians to DO something. Up to this point, he had been talking about what they believed or what they didn't have to do. Now he changes the subject to behavior. The second thing that seems to point to this being a major transition in the book is the phrase, in view of God's mercy. Since 1:18 we have been under the threat of God's wrath, but all Paul has shared about this free gift of righteousness that comes by faith in Jesus Christ is God's mercy to us.

One of the big complaints about the theology of grace is that it gives no direction. It throws holy living out the window because God loves us no matter what. Actually, the opposite is true. Paul's teaching both here and in his other epistles tried to lay a groundwork of identity and relationship that actually make holy living possible. Behavior flows out of identity. Now that we are secure in our identity as righteous children of God, we can examine our behavior and make sure it lines up. In Ephesians, Paul spent the first three chapters laying a foundation for their identity and then in 4:1 commanded them to *"live a life worthy of the calling you have received."* Loosely translated, "make sure your behavior matches your identity." He is virtually doing the same thing here.

So after all of this theological teaching, what was Paul's first command concerning behavior? I'm sure the Romans were ready to write down the "to do" list. Paul said we should offer our bodies as living sacrifices. Under the Old Covenant, animals were offered against their will as a dead sacrifice, their death covered the sin of the offerer as payment. A lot has changed. Under the New Covenant, the sacrifice God is looking for is a living sacrifice! Death is no longer necessary, because death has already occurred. Christ died to pay the price for our sin and we died with Christ (remember Romans 6-8). There will be no more dying in this system ☺. The living sacrifice is not to pay the price for sin, but to offer ourselves to God for His use in building His Kingdom. Not only is this sacrifice living, but it is holy because He has declared it holy (justified). It is acceptable because He has made us acceptable. And it is an act of worship, freely offered as a response to what God has done for us. He is not asking us to present our soul and spirit to Him while still trying to die to our flesh. He is asking for us to give Him our body, soul, and spirit that He has redeemed and made whole and alive.

The tense of the verb Paul used for offer is interesting. The other verbs he used in this passage are present tense and seem to indicate an ongoing action. But this verb is in the Greek *aorist* tense that tends to be used for something that is done once and for all. Is there a turning point in our walk with God when we finally let go of all of our striving and self-effort, all of our attempts to die to our flesh and simply surrender all to Him, trusting His grace for the outcome? If this were the case, our ongoing focus would no longer be on ourselves and how we could improve or how we could become more spiritual, it would be on Him and His Kingdom; interesting concept (Matthew 6:33).

> *Circle the phrases **do not conform** (2), **be transformed** (2), and **do not think of yourself more highly than you ought** (3). Go back and put a number one beside the phrase **offer your bodies** and then number these three phrases 2-4. Underline the phrase **renewing of your mind** (2).*

The List

So now we have a list. It's not the Ten Commandments, but it is a list of the first four behaviors Paul addressed with the church at Rome after teaching them the importance of the Gospel, righteousness by faith. Remember this list is NOT kept in order to earn righteousness or acceptance by God. This list informs us how we represent, reflect and reveal the Father to a fallen world as His righteous children.

The first command, offer your bodies, seems to be a one-time decision that becomes a turning point in a believer's journey. The other three are all in the present tense, which implies an ongoing surrender in these three areas, conformity to the world, spiritual transformation, and humility.

Jesus said that we are in the world but not of the world (John 17:14-16). We must be a part of the world in order to influence the world for Christ, but we are not to let the world press us into its mold (12:2). And we are not to fall in love with the world system (I John 2:15). The worldly system or *kosmos* is under the direct control of Satan. He uses certain schemes to keep his system running and he desires for followers of Christ to buy into his system. Selfishness, greediness, entitlement, lack of love, and passivity are all integral parts of Satan's scheme to defeat the Kingdom of God. However, Satan has also duped the church into believing that worldliness or conformity to the world is about particular sins or behaviors. As long as you don't smoke, don't drink, don't use drugs, don't engage in sex outside of marriage, and are faithful to church services and tithe, you are considered godly. The problem is that the church is **filled** with selfish, greedy, entitled, unloving, passive Christians who don't drink, smoke, engage in sex outside of marriage, and who attend church and tithe. The result is division, powerlessness and minimal impact. What would happen if we identified the schemes Satan uses in this world and refused to be pressed into their mold? God has proven that he can turn the world upside down with a few people who are loving, selfless, simple, grace-filled, and passionate about the Gospel!

The negative command *do not be conformed* has its positive counterpart in the next command: be transformed. While conformity is being pressed into shape by what is outside of us, transformation is a complete change that begins inside and slowly works itself out. It is not focused on behaviors but on character. As God transforms our character, our behaviors naturally change. This transformation happens as we renew our mind with truth. We don't need to get truth out of our head and into our heart. He gave us a good heart at the moment of salvation. We need to have our minds renewed, casting out Satan's lies and schemes and replacing them with God's truth. The result of this transformation is that we will become discerning of what **is** of God and what is **not** of God! What is God's will for my life? This question can only be answered as we refuse to buy into Satan's schemes, allow God's truth to transform our thinking, and listen for His guidance step by step.

There is something exhilarating about knowing that we are living in connection with God's spirit that lives in us. The ways of the world begin to feel foreign to us and we see life in a different way. The danger in this is that we begin to think more highly of ourselves than we should. We have arrived. We "get it" and others "don't get it." Paul's fourth command to us, also in the present tense, is that we not think too highly of ourselves. Basically he is asking us to put ourselves in perspective. We have new life because God graciously offered Christ who paid the price for our sin. We know the truth because God chose to reveal His truth to us through His Word and through His Spirit that He placed in us. If God has allowed us to understand His ways in a clearer way than others, He has a purpose for doing so, and it is NOT to make us look good or more spiritual. It is always about building His Kingdom and bringing glory to His name.

---

*Draw a square around the phrases **one body**, **many members** and **not all have the same function** (4). Highlight the words **prophesying** (6) , **serving** (7), **teaching** (7), **encouraging** (8), **contributing to needs** (8), **leadership** (8) and **showing mercy** (8).*

Spiritual Gifts

It is natural at this point for Paul to talk about spiritual gifts. Spiritual gifts are different ways that the Holy Spirit manifests Himself through a believer for the building up of the body of Christ or the expansion of His Kingdom. He makes the comparison here between the human body and the body of Christ just as he does in I Corinthians 12. Our human body is just one body, but it is made up of many different members who all have a unique purpose. The eye cannot be the hand, the mouth cannot be the foot, the nose cannot be the ear, etc. Each part of our human body is unique and each plays a specific role for the good of the whole body. Each is equally important and none are meant to be greater than others.

In the same way, God places people in His body with different abilities and passions. Each is unique and each is important. In this passage, he mentioned people who prophesy (proclaim truth), serve, teach, encourage, give, lead, and show mercy. In I Corinthians 12 and in Ephesians 4, Paul wrote similar lists that included some of these and added to it. I don't believe it was Paul's intent in these three passages to create an exhaustive list of spiritual gifts. I think he was using some generic examples of ways that God has used people to build up the body of Christ. There are probably as many spiritual gifts as there are people. Paul's point was not to pick which one of these on the list is your gift, but that whatever God gives you the ability to do, and whatever He gives you the passion to do is your role in His Kingdom. It is just as important to Him as any other role. Paul's teaching on humility evidently needed to be applied to the hierarchy of the church, which was elevating certain gifts above others. God is not in that kind of hierarchy, but knows each individual believer has something of importance to contribute to the Kingdom because His Spirit is in them and He wants to use them in a unique way. So Paul's admonition was neither to be ashamed of our gift or brag about our gift but to perform our service to the best of our ability and with love and compassion.

Several years ago we built a new auditorium at the church I was pastoring. Because of my own struggles with the flesh and my belief that all spiritual gifts are equally important, I did not want to have a high platform at the front that elevated and separated me from the people as I preached. The floor was sloped, the platform had only step and I often walked out into the crowd as I spoke. Too often those in church leadership begin to feel they are "above" others. Spiritual gifts are manifestations of the Spirit of God who is in every believer!

Questions to Ponder:

1. Explain why Romans 12:1 is called "the big therefore"?

2. Can you recall a time in your spiritual journey when you made a conscious choice to offer yourself wholly to God? How has that changed the course of your life?

3. What does God specifically desire for us in relationship to conformity to the world system?

Day 31

◆◆◆◆◆◆◆◆◆◆◆◆◆◆◆◆◆◆◆◆◆◆◆◆

What Does Righteous Living Look Like?
(Romans 12:9-21)

9 Love must be sincere. Hate what is evil; cling to what is good. 10 Be devoted to one another in brotherly love. Honor one another above yourselves. 11 Never be lacking in zeal, but keep your spiritual fervor, serving the Lord. 12 Be joyful in hope, patient in affliction, faithful in prayer. 13 Share with God's people who are in need. Practice hospitality. 14 Bless those who persecute you; bless and do not curse. 15 Rejoice with those who rejoice; mourn with those who mourn. 16 Live in harmony with one another. Do not be proud, but be willing to associate with people of low position. Do not be conceited. 17 Do not repay anyone evil for evil. Be careful to do what is right in the eyes of everybody. 18 If it is possible, as far as it depends on you, live at peace with everyone.

19 Do not take revenge, my friends, but leave room for God's wrath, for it is written: "It is mine to avenge; I will repay," says the Lord. 20 On the contrary: "If your enemy is hungry, feed him; if he is thirsty, give him something to drink. In doing this, you will heap burning coals on his head." 21 Do not be overcome by evil, but overcome evil with good.

There is a big difference between going on a hike and being a hiker. Since I am not really a hiker, if I go on a hike I need to be told exactly what to do to prepare and execute a successful hike. I might make a checklist, focus on each item and check them off as I accomplish them. The seasoned hiker on the other hand, knows intuitively how to prepare and execute a successful hike. A checklist is not needed, but a running commentary in the back of their minds reminding them of what they already know is helpful.

The passage we are studying looks a lot like a checklist. In fact, most Christians approach it as something like a continuation of the Ten Commandments. These are the things that a good Christian must DO. There is a lot of striving involved in this approach. I will admit that there is a grocery list of behaviors found in these verses, but Paul's presentation of the list doesn't appear to be a checklist to obey but a reminder of what it looks like to live out the righteousness we have received. There are actually 38 verb forms used in these 13 verses, but only six of them are written as commands. The majority of the verb forms are participles. The difference is subtle. Paul is not saying, "Do this!" he is saying "And we are doing this, and this, and this…" as if those to whom he is writing already know what living in righteousness looks like, and he is simply reminding them and encouraging them. These behaviors aren't foreign and difficult to pull off; they are the natural outflow of the righteousness of Christ that was given to us by faith.

> *Draw a bold box around the phrase **love must be sincere** (9).*

Begin With Love

How appropriate that Paul would start with love, since Jesus clearly summarized the behavior of a Christ follower with the same word (Mark 12:28-31). Even though this phrase is not an imperative, it could be said that every other behavior pointed out in this passage is an expression of sincere love. Let's look at how other translators have translated this important phrase:

"Love from the center of who you are, don't fake!" The Message
"Don't just pretend to love others. Really love them." New Living Translation
"Let love be without hypocrisy." New King James Version
"Let your love be sincere, a real thing." Amplified Bible

Our English word "sincere" comes from a Latin word that literally means "without wax." The early Roman merchants would put their pottery out to sell. If some developed cracks, the merchant would mix wax with the color of the pottery, fill in the cracks, and polish it so that the cracks were not seen. Over time, consumers learned to pick up the pottery and hold it up to the sun. The light would shine through the wax and expose the cracks. Our lives need to be honest and sincere, not necessarily without cracks but without wax.

Common to our human flesh is the desire to look good in the eyes of others or to be thought of well. Benevolent acts toward those who are in need can make someone look like a loving, caring person. The problem comes when the image is more important than the reality. Paul is setting the bar for his list of behaviors. He is not saying that Christ followers should do loving things, he is saying that those who follow Christ really LOVE, really CARE, and that it flows out of them without wax (fakeness, hypocrisy). We don't have to manufacture the love; it has already been shed abroad in our hearts (5:5).

---

*Put a number 1 beside the word **hate** (9), a number 2 beside the words **be devoted** (10), a number 3 beside the word **honor** (10), a number 4 beside the words **never be lacking in zeal**, a number 5 beside the words **be joyful** (12) and a number 6 beside the word **share** (13).*

Love Between Brothers

The overall theme of this passage is behavior, but in verses 9-13 Paul seems to be addressing six areas of behavior that specifically impact our relationships with fellow believers. The phrase "hate what is evil; cling to what is good" must be read in the context. It is not referring to our overall attitude toward good and evil, but it is specifically telling us to hate the evil in people and stick to the good that is in them. Every other phrase in this passage has to do with relationships with people, so it would be inconsistent not to connect this to people as well. This love for people is to be without hypocrisy. Because of who we are (righteous), it is hypocritical to hate a person because of their behavior since their behavior no longer defines them. It would also be hypocritical to condone evil behavior just because a person is righteous. We can separate the two and hate the evil behavior while at the same time loving the person.

This love that we have for each other, regardless of our behavior, is relational love. It is "brotherly love" because we are connected in Christ. We are all a part of His body, and we are family. Paul uses two words in this phrase that are related: *philostorgos* (be devoted) and *philadelphia* (brotherly love). The word *philos* is relational love, *storgos* is the love of a parent with a child while *adelphos* is the word for brother. The overall picture is that of a family. We love each other because we are family, all children of God through Christ.

This type of love includes honor (10). The word literally means placing a value on something. Elsewhere Paul instructs us "in lowliness of mind, esteem others better than yourselves" (Philippians 2:3). This is not something we have to try hard to do. Christ IS our life and He "made Himself nothing" so that we might be the children of God (Philippians 2:5-11). Real love is not self-centered nor is it nonchalant. Loving each other as followers of Christ is energizing, exciting, and encouraging. "Never lacking in zeal" (11) translates a verb that means sluggish or slothful. The life that is in us is ABUNDANT life, it is not sluggish but it is active and exciting. The word "fervor" (11) is actually the word for boiling water. I remember years ago working with some Jamaican migrant workers on a missions trip. While they worked they sang:

> *It's bubbling, it's bubbling, it's bubbling in my soul*
> *I'm singing, I'm dancing, since Jesus made me whole*
> *Some folks don't understand it, but I can't keep it quiet*
> *It's bubbling, bubbling, bubbling, bubbling, bubbling day and*
> *night!*

There was nothing sluggish about their singing or their love for God and each other!

Of course Paul knew that not all of life was easy and that excitement and enthusiasm doesn't characterize every day. In spite of negative circumstances though, we can be joyful because of hope, we can bear up (be patient) under affliction as we continually express our dependence on God in prayer (12). I don't know if you have ever experienced all of those together, but I know I have. I struggle with a physical condition known as lupus. It flares up regularly causing pain, fever, and can be life-threatening. I admit that sometimes I wallow in self-pity about my physical condition, but more often I am able to remember that this is not going to last forever (hope). I can praise God for what will be in the future (joy), I can keep serving Him in spite of the pain (patience), and I can whine to Him if I want to because He always listens.

If you read through the Gospels and follow the life of Christ, you often run across the phrase "moved with compassion." This phrase is used of Christ when he saw a leper, when he saw a hungry multitude, when he saw a group of diseased people, and when he saw a blind man. Jesus felt something inside when he saw someone in need, physically, emotionally, or spiritually. The response will start with a feeling (compassion) and end in action. Christ in us will respond to the needs we see in others. Sharing and being hospitable (13) flows out of Christ in us.

*Put a number 7 beside the word **bless** (14), put a number 8 beside the word **rejoice** (15), put a number 9 beside the phrase **live in harmony** (16), put a number 10 beside the phrase **do not repay** (17), put a number 11 beside the phrase **live at peace** (18), and put a number 12 beside the phrase **do not take revenge** (19).*

Loving All Men

Paul continues with his view of what it looks like to love sincerely in verses 14-21, but he seems to shift the focus to the larger group of people, not just those we are related to in Christ, but everyone. He begins by acknowledging that there are those who persecute Christians (he used to be one of them). Our persecutors may say or do mean and evil things to us, but we are not to stoop to their level, we are to be different. We can bless them (14). I don't think Paul means we should say, "good job" but we can think of something good to say about anyone, and focusing on the good will help us endure the persecution and give us the best opportunity to reach our persecutor for Christ.

Empathizing with people or sharing in their emotions, whether positive or negative, makes a connection on a heart level. Sometimes we have a difficult time connecting with the feelings of others because we are so pre-occupied with our own feelings. When Christ was hanging on the cross, enduring the agony of crucifixion, He empathized with Mary, His mother, and with the thief hanging next to Him. As we allow Christ to flow through us, we can do the same. We can rejoice and weep with others (15).

Godly relationships require humility. We all have the ability in Christ to join other people where they are, no matter how educated, articulate, rich, refined, or religious. The righteous identity we have in Christ was not given to us because we were better than anyone else. It was given as a gift, by grace. Grace levels the playing field for us all. In my travels to third-world countries, I have been honored to meet some of the most humble people. They live simply, with very little education or material possessions, but we are equal in Christ. We share the same power, the same wisdom, and the same inheritance. We can live at peace with others when we realize that we are no better or no worse than they.

No Revenge

The last phrases Paul uses all have to do with the subject of revenge. We all carry in us a sense of justice. We want things to be fair, to be equal. The problem is that our viewpoint is skewed by selfishness that is a part of our flesh. Even though we are righteous, it is difficult for us to have righteous judgment because we are limited by what we perceive. There have been many times that I have given someone a "piece of my mind" because of something they did to me or someone I loved and then later found out that I didn't have the whole story. Only God has the whole story. Don't seek to right all wrongs or make all things fair. When injustice happens, many times we have to surrender it to God and allow Him to sort it out. He will always do justly.

Three different times in this passage, Paul has touched on the subject of returning evil for evil (14, 17, 21). What if God had returned evil for evil? What if there was no such thing as grace? None of us would have a chance to have a relationship with God; we would all be condemned. Christ in us prompts us to refrain from dishing out evil to those who dish it out to us. The grace we have fully received flows through us to others, even those who cause us pain.

Questions to Ponder:

1. How can we tell the difference between sincere and insincere love?

2. Write a paragraph describing what it looks like to "love one another" according to this passage.

3. What is the key to surrendering our right for revenge?

Day 32

◆◆◆◆◆◆◆◆◆◆◆◆◆◆◆◆◆◆◆◆◆◆◆

Attitude Toward Authority
(*Romans 13:1-7*)

1 Everyone must submit himself to the governing authorities, for there is no authority except that which God has established. The authorities that exist have been established by God. 2 Consequently, he who rebels against the authority is rebelling against what God has instituted, and those who do so will bring judgment on themselves. 3 For rulers hold no terror for those who do right, but for those who do wrong. Do you want to be free from fear of the one in authority? Then do what is right and he will commend you. 4 For he is God's servant to do you good. But if you do wrong, be afraid, for he does not bear the sword for nothing. He is God's servant, an agent of wrath to bring punishment on the wrongdoer. 5 Therefore, it is necessary to submit to the authorities, not only because of possible punishment but also because of conscience. 6 This is also why you pay taxes, for the authorities are God's servants, who give their full time to governing. 7 Give everyone what you owe him: If you owe taxes, pay taxes; if revenue, then revenue; if respect, then respect; if honor, then honor.

New Hampshire's Mt. Washington may not be the highest peak in the United States (6228 feet), but it is home to some of the most severe weather in the Continental United States. A weather conservatory near the summit clocked winds of 231 miles per hour in 1932. As I am writing this chapter, a news story is breaking about a group of hikers on this mountain. Ten hikers from Pennsylvania hiked to the summit but got caught in some bad weather on their descent. The temperatures plummeted below zero quickly and the wind blew gusts of 95 mph. Four of the hikers were separated from the others and got lost in the blinding snow. They dug into the snow drifts for shelter and activated a GPS

Satellite messenger. The local forest rangers picked up the signal. Several of their strongest mountaineers set out by snow vehicle and then on foot, risking their own lives, and rescued the hikers.

Forest rangers are the police of the woods. We may get annoyed with them on occasion when they make us stick to the path, reprimand us for breaking off leaves and flowers, and even fine us for harming wildlife. The truth is that the forest rangers are there for our good. In Romans 13, Paul continued the section on behavior that flows out of this gift of righteousness. He literally described what it looks like to "not be conformed to the world" but be "transformed" (12:2). In this chapter, he instructed us about our attitude toward authority.

Circle the word **submit *(1)*, established *(1)*, rebels *(2)*, rebelling** *(2) and* **submit *(5)*.** *Draw a square around the words* **governing authority *(1)*, rulers *(3)*, God's servant *(4)*, God's servant *(4)* and God's servant *(6)*.** *Underline the words* **bear the sword *(4)* and governing *(6)*.** *Highlight the words* **judgment *(2)*, wrath *(4)*, punishment *(4)* and punishment *(5)*.**

Who?

Take a look at the way we marked this passage. The words we drew a square around represent WHO Paul was talking about. The words we underlined represent WHAT they do for us. The words we circled represent WHY we should do what Paul said and the words we highlighted tell us WHAT WILL HAPPEN if we don't.

Let's begin with who Paul was talking about in this passage. He began by calling them governing authorities (1). Other translations use the word "powers" instead. There are two major Greek words translated power in the New Testament. The first is *exousia*, the word that is used there. It is sometimes translated power, but it is literally the right or authority to exercise power. The other word is *dunamis* and is also translated power but has more to do with the ability to do something. When Paul called these people authorities, he was talking about people who have been given the right to exercise power or control over others. This authority is not theirs at birth; it was given to them by God (1) and bestowed on them by men. Remember that these Christians were living in Rome. Rome had been a monarchy, then became a republic, and was currently an empire. The ruler at the time Paul wrote this epistle was probably Nero, the fifth Roman Emperor and one of the most evil that Rome had ever known. I am sure that the church gasped when they heard Paul's words read to them the first time. Nero received his authority from God? It didn't seem possible.

Paul also called these authorities rulers (3). The word used here is the word for a leader or a master. The first term depicted their power, the second their position. Then twice in verse 4 Paul calls them servants. The word he uses both times in this verse is the word that is elsewhere translated "deacon." The government authorities are like deacons, they are servants of the people. I'm sure this was a stretch for the people at Rome. They could not imagine thinking of Nero as their servant. In verse 6, Paul changed the word used to describe these authorities again. This time he used the word that is often translated priest in the New Testament and designates someone who provides common services to help others. The government was put in place by God, given its authority by God, and was to serve the people by ministering to their everyday needs. Remember though, we live in a fallen world so it doesn't always work the way God ordained it.

As Americans, we like to think of God as the author of democracy. We may even think of God as a Democrat or a Republican or a member of the Tea Party. The truth is that God ordains government as He deems best to fit the culture of people in a particular place at a particular time in history. It is God who removes and sets up Kings (Daniel 2:11). He even puts wicked and self-centered men like Nebuchadnezzar of Babylon in power for His purposes (Daniel 4:17). Ronald Reagan, George Washington, Barack Obama, Adolf Hitler, and Idi Amin were all given authority by God to rule; sometimes to lead toward Him, sometimes to chastise. The larger point that Paul was making is that God is ultimately in charge.

Why?

This brings us to the next question; WHY? Why is there government that has power over us, and why must we submit to that government, even when it is evil? The answer lies in a small Greek word used in various forms in this passage. It is the word *tasso*. The word means to appoint, ordain, or put in order. Every word that you circled in this passage is a form of this Greek word.

First we are told to submit (1) to the governing authorities. Submit is the word *upotasso*. The prefix on the word is a preposition meaning under. We are appointed to be under the authority of the governing authorities. Those governing authorities have been established by God (1). The word established is *tasso*. God has put them in order under Himself and then we are placed under them. This chain of authority is very important. We are to obey the governing authorities as they reflect God's authority. If the two authorities come into conflict, we must obey the higher authority. This is why Jesus told the Jewish leaders to pay their taxes (Matthew 22:20), but the Spirit instructed Peter and John to preach the Gospel even though the governing authorities told them not to (Acts 4). Being under God's authority does not exempt us from human authority, unless human authority is asking us to disobey God's authority. In fact, Paul said in verse 2 if we rebel (*antitasso*) against human authority, we are rebelling (*antitasso*) against God Himself, because He has placed human authority over us. All of God's creation has an order to it. The Gospel has given us the righteousness of God apart from the law and has set us free from the laws of sin and death, but it has NOT set us free from the laws of our land. We are still subject to governing authorities. In fact, righteousness is lived out by obedience to authority.

What?

So now that we understand where we fall in relationship to this governing authority and we know that the governing authority is appointment by God to serve our needs, WHAT exactly is this government ordained to do? Paul mentioned two responsibilities of government in this passage. These are the words that you underlined. First, government bears the sword. In other words, government is ordained to protect people from evil by being given the authority to execute judgment on evildoers. The sword is a reference to judgment. All of the words you highlighted in the passage are also words of judgment. In fact, some of these very same words have been used throughout the book of Romans, starting with Romans 1:18 where Paul began talking about God's wrath that was being poured out on unrighteousness and ungodliness. However, we also learned that once we receive this righteousness that is by faith, we are no longer subject to God's wrath or condemnation (8:1). So what is all of this talk about punishment in Romans 13? This is not referring to punishment from God but punishment from human government. Christians are exempt from the wrath of God, because God poured out all of His wrath on Jesus who took our place. However, we are NOT exempt from the punishment that is the consequence of disobeying human government. If we do evil, even though we are free from condemnation, we will be subject to the "sword" of the government. Do you see Paul's larger point here? He is encouraging the Roman Christians to be model citizens BECAUSE they are righteous. This is what it looks like to be transformed by God instead of conformed to the world (12:2). We do not flaunt our freedom but we submit to authority.

The second responsibility of the government is to govern (6). They are to be vigilant, always looking out for our needs and finding new and better ways to minister to the population. Of course, governing authorities are not exempt from selfishness and greed. In the American political system, money and power have often corrupted leaders. The good news is that we have a legal right (given to us by God under the authority of the Constitution) to remove people from their position of authority. God can use us and our influence to work His will in the government. For us, living in a democratic system, being a model citizen is more than just obeying the laws of the land. It includes being involved in the election of officials and the passing of policy and law that reflects God's authority over us.

In the end, we are to know our place in God's order of authority and give to everyone what is due them by virtue of that order (7). Taxes, revenue, respect, or honor are given because it has been ordained by God Himself.

Questions to Ponder:

1. List and describe the different words Paul uses to describe those in authority.

2. What is the relationship between righteousness and obedience to authority?

3. Where are we, as Christians, to disobey human government? Give an example.

Day 33

♦♦♦♦♦♦♦♦♦♦♦♦♦♦♦♦♦♦♦♦♦♦♦♦

The Law and Love
(Romans 13:8-14)

8 Let no debt remain outstanding, except the continuing debt to love one another, for he who loves his fellowman has fulfilled the law. 9 The commandments, "Do not commit adultery," "Do not murder," "Do not steal," "Do not covet," and whatever other commandment there may be, are summed up in this one rule: "Love your neighbor as yourself." 10 Love does no harm to its neighbor. Therefore love is the fulfillment of the law. 11 And do this, understanding the present time. The hour has come for you to wake up from your slumber, because our salvation is nearer now than when we first believed. 12 The night is nearly over; the day is almost here. So let us put aside the deeds of darkness and put on the armor of light. 13 Let us behave decently, as in the daytime, not in orgies and drunkenness, not in sexual immorality and debauchery, not in dissension and jealousy. 14 Rather, clothe yourselves with the Lord Jesus Christ, and do not think about how to gratify the desires of the flesh.

Along the Appalachian Trail in the Eastern United States there are many information signs with rules and regulations posted to help protect the trail. One sign has a list of the types of vehicles not allowed on the trail: no bicycles, no motorized vehicles, no mopeds, etc. At another point of the trail, is a much simpler sign that really says the same thing; it simply states, "Foot traffic only." You have to love simplicity!

In the second half of Romans 13, Paul was posting a similar sign. As he continued with a long section on behavior that started in 12:2 with the admonition to be transformed by God's Spirit and not conformed to the world, he summed up the whole discussion by saying, love one another (13:8). In this passage Paul not only addressed the behavior of the Christians but answers the question, "What about the law now?"

Draw a box around the phrase **love one another** *(8). Circle the words* **fulfilled** *(8),* **summed up** *(9) and* **fulfillment** *(10). Underline the word* **therefore** *(10).*

Love One Another

Although the words love one another are not written as an imperative, they are connected to the phrase *let no debt remain* which is written as an imperative (8). Debt is an interesting thing. If you owe someone money, every time you meet them, the debt is the first thing you think about.   Paul wanted us to feel a debt of love toward everyone so that when we meet them, it is the first thing we think about.   The main point of this whole section is that loving one another is expected. It is not a command in the same way the Ten Commandments were.   The Ten Commandments were commands to act righteously, written to a group of people who had no resources to follow them. This command to love is written to a group of people who are the recipients of God's love and who have the love of God in them (5:5), making them fully equipped to simply be channels of God's love.

God is righteous and God is love.   These two things do not contradict each other and have not changed. God's covenant with man has changed. Under the Old Covenant mankind was held to an impossible standard that ultimately pronounced him guilty before God. Under the New Covenant, mankind is offered God's love and then asked to allow it to flow through them to others. God's standard has not changed. God is still righteous. If we act lovingly toward our neighbor, we will also act in obedience. Stealing from my neighbor would not be loving. Coveting from my neighbor would not be loving. Murdering my neighbor would not be loving.   Committing adultery with my neighbor's wife would not be loving. This is why Paul said that love sums up the whole law. If I truly love my neighbor, these laws will be obeyed. The standard is still the same, but the focus has shifted and the resources are vastly different. The focus is no longer obedience but love. The resources are not something we have to find, strive for, work up to, or earn but are given to us freely as a gift! Don't you love the New Covenant?

But love doesn't just sum up the whole law, it also fulfills the law. The word used for fulfill means to fill all the way up, even to overflowing! There is a hint in the passage that helps explain how love overflows the law. This hint is connected to the word "therefore" (10). The first part of that verse says that love does no harm to His neighbor. In other words love does good to his neighbor; therefore, love fulfills the law. For example, I could live in a right relationship with my neighbor by not murdering him, not stealing from him, not coveting his things or not committing adultery with his wife, but I still might not be a good neighbor. The law of love goes beyond the Ten Commandments and actually does good things for the neighbor. Loving my neighbor results not only in obeying the commandments, but in positive acts of love toward him. It is overflowing love.

I can almost hear Paul singing, "What the world needs now, is love, sweet love. No, not just for some, but for everyone!" Remember that Paul was writing this letter from Corinth. Corinth was known for sexual promiscuity, prostitution, and all kinds of immoral behavior. The culture there had abandoned itself to sexual pleasure in an effort to find love. Not only that, but Paul was writing to Rome. Rome at this point was a military machine ruled by a cruel and oppressive emperor. The ability to really love IS the power of the Gospel. It has the power to change the hearts of men and the power to change cultures. No wonder Paul seemed to be screaming, "Stop worrying about the Ten Commandments and LOVE!"

---

*Draw a box around the phrase **understanding the present time (11)**. Circle the phrases **put aside (12)**, **put on (12)** and **clothe yourselves (14)**. Draw a box around **do not think about how to gratify the desires of the flesh (14)**.*

Contextual Love

The second command of this passage is found in verse 11. The actual verb in the imperative tense is in the first phrase of the verse when Paul says "and do this", and it relates to the concept of understanding the present time. Paul was telling them to put the command to love in the context of their present culture and time. He was saying that time was of the essence. The salvation that is nearer (11) is the coming of Christ and the complete fulfillment of our redemption, including our bodies. It is interesting that in the first century Paul would use the word "near" to describe it. We continue to say the same things nearly 2,000 years later! The truth is that His coming is nearer than when we first believed. Scripture is clear that no one knows when Christ will return so we aren't going to waste any time trying to guess. However, we do know that His coming is one day nearer today than it was yesterday. This means we have one less day to make an impact on this world with the love that flows out of the glorious Gospel!

In light of the urgency of the hour, Paul encouraged them to put aside (12) the deeds of darkness later described in verse 13. If we take these verses out of context, we will go back to a laundry list of do's and don'ts. We must remember that this whole passage is in the context of love. Orgies, drunkenness, sexual immorality, debauchery (excessive sensual indulgence), dissension, and jealousy are all unloving. There is a conscious choice that we must make NOT to engage in these activities if our flesh leads us toward them. We don't have to overcome them, die to them, strive against them; we simply need to chose to deny them. We are already dead to them and they have no real power over us. In contrast, we are to put on (12) the armor of light. The contrast here is between the deeds of darkness and the armor of light. Darkness is representative of unrighteousness and light is righteousness. Paul used similar language in Ephesians when he writes "put off the old man" and "put on the new man" (Ephesians 4:22-24) and encourages us to "put on the whole armor of God" (Ephesians 6:11). He summarizes what he means by simply saying be clothed with the Lord Jesus Christ. Our clothes are the first thing people see when they meet us. We want people to see Jesus when they meet us. What is it about us that will reflect Jesus most clearly? It is love.

The third command of this passage is found in verse 14: do not think about how to gratify the desires of the flesh. The desires of the flesh are assumed. We all have them and we can all allow them to control us. When Paul started this discussion about behavior in 12:1-2, he said we are to be transformed (changed from the inside out) rather than conformed (pressed into the mold of the world system). In 12:2, he said that this transformation will be accomplished by the renewing of our minds. Now in 13:14, Paul is telling us that walking in righteousness and walking in love will require some mental discipline. Training our minds with truth, becoming more aware of the lies Satan sends into our minds to trigger the desires of our flesh, and setting our minds on Christ is an important part of living a righteous and loving life. All of the tools are there, we simply must choose them in the moment.

Questions to Ponder:

1. If God has not changed, what has changed now that we are under a New Covenant?

2. How does love fulfill the law?

3. What is our responsibility toward the desires of our flesh?

Day 34

♦♦♦♦♦♦♦♦♦♦♦♦♦♦♦♦♦♦♦♦♦♦♦

The Weaker Brother
(Romans 14:1-12)

1 Accept him whose faith is weak, without passing judgment on disputable matters. 2 One man's faith allows him to eat everything, but another man, whose faith is weak, eats only vegetables. 3 The man who eats everything must not look down on him who does not, and the man who does not eat everything must not condemn the man who does, for God has accepted him. 4 Who are you to judge someone else's servant? To his own master he stands or falls. And he will stand, for the Lord is able to make him stand. 5 One man considers one day more sacred than another; another man considers every day alike. Each one should be fully convinced in his own mind. 6 He who regards one day as special, does so to the Lord. He who eats meat, eats to the Lord, for he gives thanks to God; and he who abstains, does so to the Lord and gives thanks to God. 7 For none of us lives to himself alone and none of us dies to himself alone. 8 If we live, we live to the Lord; and if we die, we die to the Lord. So, whether we live or die, we belong to the Lord. 9 For this very reason, Christ died and returned to life so that he might be the Lord of both the dead and the living. 10 You, then, why do you judge your brother? Or why do you look down on your brother? For we will all stand before God's judgment seat. 11 It is written: "'As surely as I live,' says the Lord, 'every knee will bow before me; every tongue will confess to God.'" 12 So then, each of us will give an account of himself to God.

The George Washington and Jefferson Nationals Forests contain 1.8 million square acres of land in Virginia, West Virginia, and Kentucky. The forests contain 325 miles of the Appalachian Trail, 12 other trails totaling 143 miles, and 33 wilderness areas. There are large parts of the forests that have no marked trails or signage to direct hikers. If you enter the forests there are warnings that encourage hikers to stay on the trails because of the danger of getting lost. A well-seasoned and educated hiker might look with disdain on that warning and strike out off trail to a wilderness area, but the novice hiker will probably treat those warnings as one of the Ten Commandments. The experienced hiker feels freed from the warning because of what he knows, and the novice feels bound by the warning because of what he doesn't know. The warning is not really a law. You wouldn't be fined for hiking off the trail, it is simply a warning.

This same situation is present in the church. Those who are new in their faith or who haven't been taught the truths about our freedom in Christ may feel bound by certain traditional church rules and standards, while those who are more mature and have embraced the truth of our freedom in Christ may practice freedom in these areas. Though God, under the New Covenant, does still clearly define certain actions as sin (adultery, drunkenness, stealing, etc.), most of these traditional church beliefs are opinions about things that are not specifically mentioned in the *Bible* (make-up, hair length, movies, drinking alcohol, playing cards, buying a lottery ticket, etc.).

Beginning in Romans 12, Paul began addressing the behavior of those who are righteous. He urged the believers not to allow the world system to press them into its mold (conformity). Specifically, he has encouraged us to serve one another (12:4ff), love one another sincerely (12:9ff), and submit to one another (13:1ff). Now in Romans 14 and 15, Paul encouraged the members of the church at Rome to accept each other, in spite of differing opinions about certain practices.

Draw a box around the phrases **accept him whose faith is weak** *(1),* **must no look down** *(3) and* **must not condemn** *(3). Circle the word* **accept** *(1) and* **accepted** *(3) and draw a line connecting them.*

Acceptance

In the first three verses of Romans 14, there are three commands. These commands concern those who are weak in the faith. The

NIV translation of verse 1 is a little misleading. Paul is not actually addressing their personal faith but talking about their understanding of **the** faith. In relationship to the truth or doctrine of their new faith (the new covenant), they are weak or literally lacking strength. Differences in maturity as it relates to the truth can cause great division in the church, and Paul is giving some instructions to help the church at Rome avoid this problem.

When we think of opinions that divide the body of Christ in our day, we think of subjects like alcohol, dress standards, taboo activities, etc. Paul used two examples in this passage relevant to his day. The first is eating meat. Some believers were vegetarians and some were meat-eaters. The problem was related to two facts. First, many of the believers at Rome had a Jewish background. The Jews were forbidden to eat certain types of meat that were considered unclean. Upon receiving salvation, these restrictions would have been lifted, but many Jews continued to feel like it was important to avoid unclean meat. Not only that, but in the pagan culture, meat that had been offered to idols and false gods was sold in the market place, often at a reduced price. Some believers felt that eating this meat was sinful because it was associated with idolatry, while others enjoyed the cheaper prices. With both of these issues, the weaker brother would have been the one who still felt bound to the restrictions, while the more mature brother would know that God didn't really care whether they ate meat or not.

The first command is given to the more mature Christians who are instructed to accept those who are weaker. The word "accept" here means to *receive to oneself* and is used for inviting someone into the home. The picture is one of throwing the door wide open, embracing the individual and inviting him in. It is the same word used in verse 3 and in 15:7 about God's acceptance of us, so it is not a grudging or a partial acceptance but a full acceptance. Paul completes the command by urging them to accept the weaker brother no matter what *disputable matter* may be an area of disagreement. Some Christians worship with their hands up and some stand stoically. Some believe that a glass of wine with dinner is perfectly fine, while others believe in total abstinence.

Dancing, movies, versions of the *Bible*, and hymns *versus* praise songs, are to be accepted by our brothers and sisters in Christ without judging their opinions or arguing. It feels like this admonition is completely ignored in the American church. Churches split, denominations isolate from others, and Christians refuse to cooperate with each other to build the Kingdom of God because of differences over matters that are not found anywhere in the *Bible*. Evidently this is not just a 21st century problem because Paul was addressing it in the first century.

Esteem

The second command actually takes the first command to another level. Not only are we to accept our brothers and sisters who have different opinions, but we are not to esteem them any less because of their opinion. The phrase "must not look down" is actually used of Christ who was the stone that the builders *rejected* (Acts 4:11). In other words, to look down upon those who have different opinions than ours is the same as rejecting them. Rejection hurts and births discord and division. These commands flow well from Paul's teaching in the first part of this book. We are all equal in God's eyes because we stand completely in His grace, so He does not esteem one believer better than another based on behavior. He accepts us all fully. In the same way, we are to look at each other, with all of our differences and idiosyncrasies, as equal by the grace of God.

The third command actually addressed the weaker brother in this relationship. If the more mature believer is accepting and not thinking less of the weaker brother, then the weaker brother is commanded not to condemn or judge the more mature believer. The way that these opinions divide the body of Christ involves the man who rolls his eyes at his brother who won't join him in smoking a nice cigar, as well as the one who is judging his brother for smoking the cigar. In other words, there is room in the body of Christ for both opinions. As Paul commanded, loving each other, serving each other, and submitting to each other involve a mutual respect that tolerates these kinds of differences.

> *Put a number 1 beside the phrase **who are you to judge** (4), a number 2 beside the phrase **each one should be fully convinced** (5), a number 3 beside the phrase for **none of us lives to himself** (7) and a number 4 beside the phrase **for this very reason**. Circle the words **look down** (10) and connect them to the same words in verse 3. Underline **the Lord is able to make him stand** (4) and **we will all stand** (10).*

The Reasoning

Paul didn't make these commands without explaining his reasoning. In verses 4-12, he lists four reasons for his three admonitions. The first reason not to judge others for their opinions is that we are not responsible for another man's servant. The master of that servant will be the judge as to whether that servant will stand or fall. We are not the master of our brothers and sisters, God is. They will stand before God and He will judge whether they stand or fall. The good news is He makes us all stand (4).

The second reason is that these opinions are a matter of the heart and are driven by our own history, our physical and emotional makeup, and our culture. Because of these we all have the freedom to decide in our heart how God feels about these subjects, and being fully persuaded, to behave accordingly. Since we cannot be fully persuaded for another, we keep our opinion to ourselves and live it out before God with a clear conscience.

Paul also indicates that relationship trumps opinions. We belong to the Lord and we don't live to ourselves, we are part of the body of Christ. Since none of these opinions affects God's ownership of us nor the fact that we are brothers and sisters, they should play a much less significant role in the church. When we get to Heaven, living with each other in the presence of God, none of these things will matter.

Finally, Paul emphasizes that only Christ is able to judge. The rest of us are all equal by God's grace and cannot stand above and look down on anyone. Everyone will be judged as equal by God Himself. We will stand before His judgment and not fall because He will make us stand (4). This is not referring to a time when we will stand before God and answer for all of our behaviors. We will stand before God in the righteousness of Christ that we received by grace through faith, and in spite of our behavior, we will be made to stand. Judgment has already happened for us. It happened on the cross, as Paul says here *for this reason Christ died and returned to life* so that we could all *stand before His judgment seat* and *give an account*.

It does sometimes seem to be a favorite sport amongst Christians to criticize and judge each other based on our opinions about certain cultural and community topics. The overall message of this passage is that God has accepted us all in spite of our quirks so we should accept each other.

Questions to Ponder:

1. How have you experienced discord and division based on differing opinions amongst believers?

2. How might things have turned out differently if the truths of Romans 14 were applied?

3. Can you say you accept others and esteem them in spite of differences of opinions?

Day 35

♦♦♦♦♦♦♦♦♦♦♦♦♦♦♦♦♦♦♦♦♦♦♦

The Danger of Judging
(Romans 14:13-23)

13 Therefore let us stop passing judgment on one another. Instead, make up your mind not to put any stumbling block or obstacle in your brother's way. 14 As one who is in the Lord Jesus, I am fully convinced that no food is unclean in itself. But if anyone regards something as unclean, then for him it is unclean. 15 If your brother is distressed because of what you eat, you are no longer acting in love. Do not by your eating destroy your brother for whom Christ died. 16 Do not allow what you consider good to be spoken of as evil. 17 For the kingdom of God is not a matter of eating and drinking, but of righteousness, peace and joy in the Holy Spirit, 18 because anyone who serves Christ in this way is pleasing to God and approved by men. 19 Let us therefore make every effort to do what leads to peace and to mutual edification. 20 Do not destroy the work of God for the sake of food. All food is clean, but it is wrong for a man to eat anything that causes someone else to stumble. 21 It is better not to eat meat or drink wine or to do anything else that will cause your brother to fall. 22 So whatever you believe about these things keep between yourself and God. Blessed is the man who does not condemn himself by what he approves. 23 But the man who has doubts is condemned if he eats, because his eating is not from faith; and everything that does not come from faith is sin.

There are some great hiking trails near Foxfire Mountain just outside of Pigeon Forge and Gatlinburg, Tennessee. One of the highlights of this area is the 400-foot-long swinging bridge that connects the base camp at Foxfire Mountain with Prosperity Mountain and bridges Dunn's Gorge. It is often referred to as the Bridge to Prosperity, and by many accounts is the longest swinging bridge in America. It is interesting to watch as people approach the bridge. Some stride confidently across, and even see how much they can make the bridge move as they go. Others approach timidly, inch forward holding tightly to the cables, startled at each tiny movement. It is reported that some have even crawled across. The truth is that the cables which support the Bridge to Prosperity are strong enough to hold 135,000 pounds, which is the equivalent of six school buses loaded with children. It is not going to fall! Fear of heights, experience or lack thereof, and past trauma affect the way people approach the bridge.

In his commentary on Romans 14, Ray Stedman compares the Christian's approach to questionable things to the way people approach the swinging bridge. Some, who are confident in their freedom in Christ and the fact that all of our sin was judged at the cross, have no problem with some of these gray areas. Others, who are not as well acquainted with grace or true identity in Christ, continue to fear that they are defined by their behaviors and are extremely cautious about what they will and won't participate in. It is not wrong to run across the swinging bridge, and it is not wrong to crawl across the swinging bridge. But it is wrong to swing the bridge when someone is crawling across it! This is the theme of the second half of Romans 14.

---

*Circle the words **judgment** (13), **make up your mind** (13), **condemn** (22) and **condemned** (23).*

Judging

Paul had just assured us in the first part of this chapter that God is the one who does the judging, and that we will be able to stand at the judgment because of what Christ has done for us. Now he begins to talk about the Christian's tendency to judge each other. This part of the discussion starts with the word *therefore,* so we don't want to separate it from the previous part of the chapter. BECAUSE God is the judge, we are encouraged not to "pass judgment on one another" (13). The Greek word for judge used here is *krino.* It means to share an opinion about whether something is right or wrong. In other words, it is not our job to go around telling other people that what they are doing is right or wrong. The Lord is the judge. The first part of verse 13 is a summary of what Paul had already taught in 14:1-12. He basically taught us what NOT to do in regards to questionable things: don't condemn or criticize others and don't try to regulate others with rules and regulations. In the second part of verse 13, Paul introduced us to what we CAN do in regards to questionable things by using the word *instead*. The phrase *make up your mind* is actually a repeat of the word *krino* or judge. We could paraphrase this verse this way, "don't judge others behavior but judge this, don't cause a brother to stumble." We are discouraged from giving others our opinion about whether a questionable thing is right or wrong, but we are encouraged to love our brothers and sisters by not causing them to stumble. Remember that this whole section about behavior is written in the context of loving one another.

Romans 14:14-21 illustrates the problem by using the example of meat offered to idols, a practice that was neither forbidden nor immoral (see Day 34). Some Christians felt completely free to eat the meat, while others felt it was wrong because of the association with idolatry. Paul concluded that discussion in 14:22-23 by returning to the topic of judging. Paul pronounced the man blessed that does not condemn (judge-*krino*) himself by what he approves. In other words, if you abstain from eating meat offered to idols when you are in the company of those who believe it is wrong, don't condemn yourself for eating it when you are not in the company of anyone that would stumble. If we are not sure if something is morally right or wrong and we participate in it, we condemn (judge-*krino*) ourselves because we are not being consistent with what we believe and thus it is not of faith (23).

---

*Draw a box around the words **stumbling block** (13), **distressed** (15), **destroy** (15), **spoken of as evil** (16), **destroy** (20), **stumble** (20) and **fall** (21).*

Stumbling

Our behavior toward our brothers and sisters is to be characterized by love and honor (12:9-10). So if my brother or sister believes they are sinning if they eat meat that is offered to idols (or goes to a movie, has a drink of wine, etc.) the loving thing for me to do is to abstain from the meat while I am in their presence. I don't have to agree with them that it is wrong, but I don't want to encourage them to eat it because their belief would make it wrong for them. If they ate the meat because I was eating the meat, they would feel guilty afterwards. I would have caused them to stumble in their walk with Christ or put up an obstacle to their progress in relationship with Him. Paul actually used a progression of words to describe the effect flaunting our liberty can have on a brother or sister. It causes them to stumble (13), it distresses them (15), and can even destroy them (15) and cause them to fall (21). Stumbling is causing them to consider sinning against their own conscience; distressing is causing them to be uneasy; destroying is causing their ruin, and falling is to be rendered powerless.

As you read that last paragraph, you might be thinking that it is a bit of an overstatement. How can our participation in a certain questionable behavior be so devastating to a fellow believer? Let me illustrate by using the example of alcohol. If you have a fellow believer who has struggled with an addiction to alcohol all of his life, it will be hard for him to practice his freedom in Christ with regard to alcohol. He or she has built up an addictive flesh pattern that sometimes doesn't go away. I am certainly free to invite him to a bar for a drink, but this practice of my freedom would cause him to stumble, make him uneasy, and may even cause him to sin against his own conscience by taking a drink which could lead him back into his addictive pattern. Of course this example is extreme, but it does illustrate the point. We do not have to restrict all of our behavior based on the opinions and whims of others, but we do have to temper all of our behaviors with love. Being sensitive to the weakness, immaturity, or flesh struggle of another and adjusting our actions to minister to their need is the loving thing to do.

It is not only the weaker brother or sister that is at risk here. It is also the Gospel itself. It is possible for the conflict over questionable things to become so divisive that the world begins to see the Gospel as a set of rules and regulations that the Christians themselves can't even agree on. In verse 16, Paul spoke of allowing something good to be spoken of as evil. That phrase *spoken of as evil* is actually the word for blaspheme. Later in verse 20, Paul admonished us not to destroy the work of God for the sake of food. God is at work in this world through His people, the church, who are indwelled by His Holy Spirit. When that work is sidetracked by quarreling over behaviors that don't really matter in light of eternity, the work of God is destroyed. This is a different Greek word for destroy than the one we saw in verse 15. This one literally means to dissolve, disunite, or deprive of success. Paul's warning is certainly applicable to the church in post-modern America. Disunity and dissolution of fellowship amongst believers is usually attributed to differences over these questionable matters, which is exactly what Paul was warning against.

> *Highlight all of verse 17, underlining the words **righteousness, peace** and **joy**. Underline the words **peace** and **mutual edification** (19).*

Missing the Point

Arguing and causing division over meat offered to idols and similar subjects could be called adventures in missing the point. The Kingdom of God is not about these behaviors; it is about righteousness. Paul had already explained that it isn't our righteousness at all, it is Christ's righteousness. He also explained that this righteousness is not earned by our behaviors, but is given to us as a free gift. His righteousness means we are as we should be; we are as He created us to be. This means that we are both pleasing to God and approved by men (18) regardless of whether or not we eat meat offered to idols. When we begin to emphasize these other things, we lose sight of the righteousness which is by faith and get focused on our behaviors which leads us right back to the law, judgment, and condemnation. On the other hand, focusing on the free gift of righteousness leads to peace and mutual edification (19).

Besides righteousness, Paul described the Kingdom of God with the words *peace* and *joy*. Both of these are considered evidence or fruit of the Spirit of God in us. Because we are righteous, God's Spirit is free to live in us and manifest Himself through us. Evidence of the Spirit in us comes out as peace and joy, not quarrels and condemnation. It is easy for us to get caught up in discussions and disagreements that don't really matter. When this happens, go back to Paul's words in Romans 14:17 and remember the point. Don't miss it!

Questions to Ponder:

1. How does judging violate love?

2. How does judging hurt the Kingdom of God?

3. How is judging like an adventure in missing the point?

Day 36

◆◆◆◆◆◆◆◆◆◆◆◆◆◆◆◆◆◆◆◆◆◆◆

More on the Weaker Brother
(Romans 15:1-13)

1 We who are strong ought to bear with the failings of the weak and not to please ourselves. 2 Each of us should please his neighbor for his good, to build him up. 3 For even Christ did not please himself but, as it is written: "The insults of those who insult you have fallen on me." 4 For everything that was written in the past was written to teach us, so that through endurance and the encouragement of the Scriptures we might have hope. 5 May the God who gives endurance and encouragement give you a spirit of unity among yourselves as you follow Christ Jesus, 6 so that with one heart and mouth you may glorify the God and Father of our Lord Jesus Christ. 7 Accept one another, then, just as Christ accepted you, in order to bring praise to God. 8 For I tell you that Christ has become a servant of the Jews on behalf of God's truth, to confirm the promises made to the patriarchs 9 so that the Gentiles may glorify God for his mercy, as it is written: "Therefore I will praise you among the Gentiles; I will sing hymns to your name." 10 Again, it says, "Rejoice, O Gentiles, with his people." 11 And again, "Praise the Lord, all you Gentiles, and sing praises to him, all you peoples." 12 And again, Isaiah says, "The Root of Jesse will spring up, one who will arise to rule over the nations; the Gentiles will hope in him." 13 May the God of hope fill you with all joy and peace as you trust in him, so that you may overflow with hope by the power of the Holy Spirit.

As we get near the end of a long trail, it is a courtesy to check in with our fellow hikers to see if everyone still has the strength and stamina to keep going. If we are more experienced at hiking, it may be easy for us to keep pressing forward without thinking about the weaker or the slower member of our group. In today's passage, Paul reminds us to do the same thing spiritually. Not everyone that we worship with or fellowship with has the same spiritual knowledge or stamina that we do. It is a courtesy and builds unity when we consider others above ourselves.

> *Circle the words **bear** (1), **build him up** (2) and the three occurrences of the word **please** (1, 2, 3). Underline **even Christ** (3) and **it is written** (3).*

Accommodate

The first part of Romans 15 is Paul's conclusion concerning how to handle questionable topics that often divide Christians. Again, he appeals to those who are stronger (spiritually) to bear or carry the burden of the immaturity of others. The word *failings* used in verse 1 is a bit misleading as a translation of the word weakness or impotence. The weak have not done anything wrong, they are just weak. It is interesting that Paul used the concept of bearing or carrying the weight of the weak. The law is burdensome, and when we limit our freedom in order to minister to people who still see themselves as under the law, it is burdensome. We long to rejoice in our freedom and focus on the positive aspects of our relationship with God rather than discuss and restrict ourselves by the opinions of others. However, this burden is sometimes necessary for us to carry as a vital part of loving one another.

Years ago I was invited to speak at a camp that believed the King James Version was the only reliable translation. They also believed that it was immodest to wear shorts. My first reaction to these limitations was not positive. It would be much more difficult to preach out of the King James Version, especially to teenagers. The temperature was going to be in the high 90's, I wanted to wear shorts. I felt the burden of these limitations but lived under them for that week in order to love the teenagers and workers and be able to communicate God's love to them. I certainly had the freedom to use the NIV and wear my Bermuda shorts but my goal was to build them up, not flaunt my freedom. It was not the time nor the place to teach them their freedom from these things.

In I Corinthians 13, Paul taught us that love is not self-seeking (I Corinthians 13:5). Sometimes loving our brother and sister means pleasing them and not ourselves. The word that Paul uses for pleasing means "to accommodate." This may help you understand what Paul was asking us to do, make accommodations for those who are weak and don't simply accommodate yourself. Some time ago, I met for dinner with a group of Christian brothers at an Italian restaurant. I personally don't feel you can enjoy good Italian food without a nice glass of Pinot Noir! Without thinking, I ordered a glass and then noticed that those around me had grown quiet. It only took me a moment to remember that the brother sitting across from me at the table had struggled with an addiction to alcohol all of his life, and it had cost him his family and his job. It was not a sin for me to order wine, but it was definitely unloving to my brother. I have also been on the receiving end of this accommodation in regards to my own struggle with addiction and know that it really ministers and communicates love.

This practice of bearing the burden of the weak and pleasing the other is for their good and their edification. Building another brother up does not mean that I agree and promote his adherence to the law, because that would not be for his ultimate good. It does mean that I accommodate in love and look for opportunities to teach about our true identity and freedom in Christ. So how long do we accommodate? The verbs **bear** and **please** that Paul uses are in the present tense. While we live in this world, we will always be confronted with these issues and must always be ready to accommodate others for their good.

Even though this is a bit of a burden, let's not forget that the ultimate burden was borne for us. Paul used the phrase "even Christ". This was written to remind us that on many occasions Christ chose to accommodate us, even taking insults, ridicule, torture, and death. Jesus practiced this principle in perfect balance. When the Pharisees tried to stop him from healing on the Sabbath because it violated the law, He did not give in because the greater good was served by healing (Matthew 12). But when they asked him about paying their taxes, He accommodated the culture because rebelling against government was not the point (Luke 20).

---

*Circle the words **accept one another** (7) and **overflow with hope** (13). Underline the words just as (7), **confirm the promises made to the patriarchs** (8), **as it is written** (9). Highlight the words **endurance** and **encouragement** (4,5) and the words joy and **peace** (13).*

Accept

Bearing with, pleasing, and building up will all be easier if we follow Paul's imperative in verse 7. *Accept one another* is a strong command instructing us to take each other in as companions. We are connected through Christ and His Spirit that is in us, and we are walking together through this life. This acceptance goes beyond simply tolerating each other. We are to accept just as Christ accepted us, with all of our imperfections, idiosyncrasies, weaknesses, and annoying habits. The rest of this passage proves that God is glorified when His people accept each other and live in unity. This kind of unity will require both endurance and encouragement (4,5). Endurance is the ability to bear up under pressure while pressing forward and encouragement is the comfort of knowing that we don't walk alone. We have both of these things in the Scriptures and in the Holy Spirit. The Scriptures give us examples and truths that help us look past our own struggles and know that we are part of something bigger than ourselves. The Holy Spirit makes sure that we know we are not alone on this journey because He walks beside us as our Comforter.

Paul masterfully integrates his teaching from the first part of Romans into this teaching about Christian behavior in community. We can accept each other because that is what the Gospel is all about, acceptance and unity. God had promised Abraham that he would become a great nation and that all of the nations of the world (including Gentiles) would be blessed through him. Christ came as a servant in response to God's promise to Abraham and has made one body out of Jews and Gentiles in order to create one heart and one spirit that can glorify and praise the Father. This is the Gospel, reconciling both Jew and Gentile to God and to each other. Again, Paul used Old Testament quotations from Psalm 18:49, Deuteronomy 32:43, Psalm 117:1, and Isaiah 11:10 to show that this was always God's plan.

As we join together in unity with our brothers and sisters from all backgrounds and beliefs and glorify God together, the Spirit in us resonates and fills us with joy, peace, and hope. Remember that in Romans 14, Paul said that the Kingdom of God was not meat and drink but righteousness, peace, and joy. Loving others enough to accept them in spite of their weaknesses and joining together as one body equipped with a righteousness that comes by faith will fill us with peace and joy. The end result is hope. A confident expectation that what God promised, He will fulfill. It will all be okay in the end. So if it isn't okay, it is not the end.

Paul closed this section on doubtful or questionable things with verse 13. He started this whole passage about Christian behavior by reminding us that love is the driving force for our behavior. So, when we are confronted with a choice about whether to participate in something that might offend another, we can choose to please our brother rather than ourselves because we love them without agreeing to put everyone back into the bondage of the law.

Questions to Ponder:

1. What is your first reaction to the limitations of walking with a weaker brother? How does this passage address those reactions?

2. How did Christ model a perfect balance between freedom and accommodations?

3. What does it look like to "accept one another"?

Day 37

♦♦♦♦♦♦♦♦♦♦♦♦♦♦♦♦♦♦♦♦♦♦♦♦

Praise and Reminders
(Romans 15:14-22)

14 I myself am convinced, my brothers, that you yourselves are full of goodness, complete in knowledge and competent to instruct one another. 15 I have written you quite boldly on some points, as if to remind you of them again, because of the grace God gave me 16 to be a minister of Christ Jesus to the Gentiles with the priestly duty of proclaiming the gospel of God, so that the Gentiles might become an offering acceptable to God, sanctified by the Holy Spirit. 17 Therefore I glory in Christ Jesus in my service to God. 18 I will not venture to speak of anything except what Christ has accomplished through me in leading the Gentiles to obey God by what I have said and done-- 19 by the power of signs and miracles, through the power of the Spirit. So from Jerusalem all the way around to Illyricum, I have fully proclaimed the gospel of Christ. 20 It has always been my ambition to preach the gospel where Christ was not known, so that I would not be building on someone else's foundation. 21 Rather, as it is written: "Those who were not told about him will see, and those who have not heard will understand." 22 This is why I have often been hindered from coming to you.

As we near the end of this trail we have been walking together, our familiarity with each other has grown and the conversation turns a little more personal. We are aware that we will be parting company soon, and we want to encourage each other, perhaps share a few things we haven't touched on yet, and remind each other of the important things we have touched on.

> *Circle the phrases **full of goodness** (14), **complete in knowledge** (14) and **competent to instruct each other** 14). Draw a box around the phrases **remind you of them again** (15), **priestly duty** (16), **proclaiming the gospel** (16) and **sanctified by the Holy Spirit** (16).*

Praise

Paul wants to end his time with the church at Rome with some praise. It must have felt good to read these words from the Apostle Paul himself. First, Paul affirmed them as full of goodness. The word for full used here refers to the condition of being full; we are all full of something! Paul believed that these followers of Christ were full of goodness, and in effect, goodness flowed from them. The motive for their actions toward each other, toward the unsaved, toward Paul, and toward God was a good motive. This is a high complement. I wonder if people can say the same of us? We don't exhibit goodness by trying to be good. We exhibit goodness because we have allowed the goodness of God to fill us up and it flows out to others.

Secondly, Paul praised them for being filled with knowledge. This word for full is a different word and emphasizes the process of being full. Picture a pitcher that is being filled with water. When the water reaches the top, the pitcher is full. The Roman believers were teachable. They were open to God's truth, and the result was that they were filled with knowledge. I would rather teach 1 ignorant person who has a teachable spirit than 100 wise people who are unteachable. When it comes to the knowledge of God, as Paul said in 11:33, it is *unsearchable*, it has no end, so we must always remain teachable and be filling up with knowledge.

Third, Paul mentions their ability to counsel each other. The word used for instruct is the Greek word *noutheteo*, which means to admonish, warn, or confront. There is a whole style of counseling termed "nouthetic" using this concept. In this form of counseling, the counselor confronts the counselee with the issues, pushing toward a resolution. Paul was praising the Roman believers for having the boldness to confront each other and work toward solutions to problems rather than to allow things to continue in passivity. Sometimes our flesh tendency is to leave things alone and hope they work themselves out. Such is not usually the case though, and loving confrontation can solve a multitude of problems.

After praising them, Paul reminded them of his purpose in writing to them. First he told them that though they were full of knowledge, they needed a bold reminder of some truths. This reiterates the earlier point that we must always remain teachable. The world system, our own flesh, and the enemy are constantly bombarding our minds with lies and deception. Renewing our minds daily (12:2) is important. We can't be certain which things Paul felt they needed to be boldly reminded of, but I am fairly sure that one of them was the righteousness that comes by faith. Since our whole disposition toward relationship with God changes based on our view of righteousness (Old Covenant or New Covenant, law or grace), he spent much time (and ink) driving this point home.

Paul also reminded them that he had provided them priestly ministry. The Jewish believers would have been very familiar with the role of the priest: to assist people to connect with the presence of God. Paul knew that people can only connect with the presence of God through the Gospel, the death burial, and resurrection of Christ. He saw his ministry of preaching the Gospel as a priestly one. It would probably be good for us to think of sharing the Gospel as a priestly duty as well. We are called a royal priesthood (I Peter 2:9) and have the privilege (and commission) to preach the Gospel to every creature (Mark 16:15).

More specifically, because of his calling as a light to the Gentiles (1:5), Paul wrote to them in order to assist the Gentile believers to experience the fullness of God's Spirit in them. A fullness that was not dependent on the law, but would flow out of the righteousness they received by faith. If righteousness had come by the law, the Jews would have had a corner on the market of the fullness of the Spirit. However, Paul was clear that righteousness comes by faith and is available equally to all. If we have received the Gospel by faith, the Spirit of God lives in us and can manifest His fullness through us. Don't let anyone tell you that your heritage, your race, your denomination, or even your behavior hinders your ability to experience the fullness of God's Spirit. This experience is life to the fullest (John 10:10).

> *Highlight the phrases **service to God** (17), what **Christ has accomplished through me** (18), **fully proclaimed the gospel of Christ** (19) and **where Christ was not known** (20).*

Reminder

We have to admire the way Paul wrote. First he praised his fellow travelers, and then he reminded them of his role. They were probably quite impressed with Paul by the end of this book and may have sought to please him or be known as one of his followers. He wanted them to know that what he had done was not to promote himself, but was a service to God. His calling came from the Father, and pointed people to the Father. In our current culture of Christian celebrities, I wonder if this same thing is true. Paul went on to remind them that what had been accomplished (the great spread of the Gospel to the Gentile world) was not accomplished because of Paul's expert planning. It was accomplished by Christ through Paul. He mentioned signs and wonders that were used to confirm the message of the Gospel. These miraculous things recorded through the book of Acts that accompanied Paul's ministry were clearly not evidence of Paul's power but of God's power. We get a glimpse at the enormity of his ministry when he mentioned the spread of the Gospel from Jerusalem to Illyricum (19). Of course Jerusalem is in Israel and Illyricum is a reference to a kingdom on the west side of the Balkan Peninsula, above modern-day Albania (a distance of over 1000 miles).

It is interesting that Paul didn't report on the success of his ministry by telling how many converts, how many churches established, or even how far he traveled. He summarized his ministry by saying that he fully proclaimed the Gospel of Christ. This is our calling. We are not called to win multitudes to Christ, change the culture, build big ministries, overthrow governments, or change the world. We are called to preach the Gospel. God does the rest. When we get confused about this, we begin to build the Kingdom of man rather than the Kingdom of God.

Paul had a particular burden for people who had not been reached. He got a special blessing from showing up in a town or city where the Gospel had not been preached and being the first one to share such good news. His desire to reach the unreached had even hindered him from being able to fulfill his desire of visiting Rome. The reason reaching the unreached was so exciting to him was because he considered the good news to be VERY good news and he wanted to be the first one to tell them!

Paul began this section by pointing to Christ as the one who was glorified by all that had been accomplished. He had a balanced opinion of who he was, neither elevating himself above others, or debasing himself. He was called by God and privileged to be used by Him.

Questions to Ponder:

1. What if Paul were writing to you. What might he have said about your goodness, knowledge and ability to instruct?

2. What specific things did Paul do to fulfill his calling as a minister of Christ Jesus?

3. What truths do you need to be reminded of regularly?

Day 38

♦♦♦♦♦♦♦♦♦♦♦♦♦♦♦♦♦♦♦♦♦♦♦♦

Future Travels
(Romans 15:23-33)

23 But now that there is no more place for me to work in these regions, and since I have been longing for many years to see you, 24 I plan to do so when I go to Spain. I hope to visit you while passing through and to have you assist me on my journey there, after I have enjoyed your company for a while. 25 Now, however, I am on my way to Jerusalem in the service of the saints there. 26 For Macedonia and Achaia were pleased to make a contribution for the poor among the saints in Jerusalem. 27 They were pleased to do it, and indeed they owe it to them. For if the Gentiles have shared in the Jews' spiritual blessings, they owe it to the Jews to share with them their material blessings. 28 So after I have completed this task and have made sure that they have received this fruit, I will go to Spain and visit you on the way. 29 I know that when I come to you, I will come in the full measure of the blessing of Christ. 30 I urge you, brothers, by our Lord Jesus Christ and by the love of the Spirit, to join me in my struggle by praying to God for me. 31 Pray that I may be rescued from the unbelievers in Judea and that my service in Jerusalem may be acceptable to the saints there, 32 so that by God's will I may come to you with joy and together with you be refreshed. 33 The God of peace be with you all. Amen.

As we draw to the end of a long trail, only the hiking enthusiast would be ready to talk about the next hike. Most people would be thinking more about a little rest and relaxation that didn't involve walking or backpacks! Paul had been travelling the world for years but he was still excited about places he hadn't been. He never stopped dreaming about reaching new places with the gospel, even though some of his dreams were never realized.

> *Underline the words* **no more place for me to work in these regions** *(23),* **Spain** *(24),* **Jerusalem** *(25) and* **Macedonia and Achaia** *(25).*

Travel Plans

Paul continued his personal conversation with the Roman believers by sharing his travel plans. He just finished telling them about his passion to reach the people who had not heard the Gospel. He felt that he had covered as much territory as he could in this region and needed to move further west, all of the way to Spain. Though he had a desire to see the Roman Christians, seeing them was going to be secondary to taking the Gospel to Spain. Rome just happened to be on the way.

Even though Paul was passionate about reaching new people groups with the Gospel, he also had an obligation to those who had supported him and who had originally sent him. The church at Jerusalem was in difficult circumstances and Paul, feeling an obligation to show honor to them as the sending group, had collected an offering in the Balkan provinces of Macedonia and Achaia and had promised to personally deliver this money to the church at Jerusalem. His passion did not cause him to be blind to those who taught him and supported him or to lose sight of his desire to connect the different churches with each other. Because of this, Paul chose to return to Jerusalem before setting off for Spain.

Paul arrived in Jerusalem on his fifth and final visit (Acts 21:17ff) around 57 AD with the offering he had collected from the saints in Macedonia and Achaia. Acts reports that he was warmly received. The Jews in Jerusalem had heard of Paul's teaching among the Gentiles and they did not respond positively. He was said to be teaching all the Jews living among the Gentiles to forsake Moses, to stop circumcising their children and that it was unnecessary to observe the customs (Acts 21:21). Isn't it human nature to resist change in spite of the good that is happening? The opposition was so fierce that Paul's life was in danger and he chose to be taken into Roman custody to avoid being killed by the Jews. When a plot to kill Paul on his way to an appearance before the Jews was discovered, he was transported by night to Caesarea. He was held as a prisoner there for two years, until a new governor reopened his case in 59 AD. When the governor suggested that he be sent back to Jerusalem for further trial, Paul exercised his right as a Roman citizen to "appeal unto Caesar." After a harrowing escape from a shipwreck on the way, Paul arrived in Rome in 60 AD and while under house arrest for two years awaiting trial, preached the Gospel and encouraged the believers. It is doubtful that Paul ever made it to Spain. After his trial, most historians believed he was martyred in Rome for his faith.

The historical record of the book of Acts and later historians confirm that even Paul did not get to realize the full extent of the ministry he envisioned. In spite of his limitations, he never stopped dreaming.

> *Highlight the words **join me** (30), **by praying** (30), **pray** (31) and **rescued from the unbelievers** (31).*

Enlisting Partners

So, at the end of this trail, Paul shared with us his plan to continue on to another trail, one that he hoped would one day allow him to meet up with us again. However, Paul was well aware that our plans are not always God's plans. He was also making these plans with full knowledge of the dangers. As was just shared, Paul met with some great obstacles when he got to Jerusalem. Before leaving for that city, he was asking these Roman believers, people he had never met, to be a part of his travels. They joined him on this journey, not by actually traveling with him, but by praying for him about the obstacles and for God's protection and guidance. What a privilege we have in joining others who minister for Christ in far away lands by praying for them and with them. We must never forget that there is an enemy who wants to thwart all attempts at spreading the Gospel and who will stand against us with great strength and power. We need the power of God and the unity of the saints to combat this enemy. Someone has said that when we share our faults with each other we no longer carry our burden alone, but others join us. In Galatians Paul told us to "bear one another's burdens and so fulfill the law of Christ." He was giving the Roman believers a chance to help him bear the burden of reaching the lost with the gospel.

In the end, Paul did get to visit the saints at Rome. He did not get to go in joy and peace, but rather in chains. Paul did not need for life to be a "happily ever after" story. He simply wanted to be a part of what God was doing in the world and experience the fullness of God's spirit flowing through him while making an impact on the lives of others.

Questions to Ponder:

1. Why would Paul risk going back to Jerusalem when he felt so strongly about reaching those who had never heard the gospel?

2. How have you participated in the ministry of the gospel by praying for someone else?

3. Are you willing to serve God even if it means things don't work out the way you envision them? What might you need to surrender to get to this point?

Day 39

♦♦♦♦♦♦♦♦♦♦♦♦♦♦♦♦♦♦♦♦♦♦

Greetings
(Romans 16:1-16)

1 I commend to you our sister Phoebe, a servant of the church in Cenchrea. 2 I ask you to receive her in the Lord in a way worthy of the saints and to give her any help she may need from you, for she has been a great help to many people, including me. 3 Greet Priscilla and Aquila, my fellow workers in Christ Jesus. 4 They risked their lives for me. Not only I but all the churches of the Gentiles are grateful to them. 5 Greet also the church that meets at their house. Greet my dear friend Epenetus, who was the first convert to Christ in the province of Asia. 6 Greet Mary, who worked very hard for you. 7 Greet Andronicus and Junias, my relatives who have been in prison with me. They are outstanding among the apostles, and they were in Christ before I was. 8 Greet Ampliatus, whom I love in the Lord. 9 Greet Urbanus, our fellow worker in Christ, and my dear friend Stachys. 10 Greet Apelles, tested and approved in Christ. 11 Greet Herodion, my relative. Greet those in the household of Narcissus who are in the Lord. 12 Greet Tryphena and Tryphosa, those women who work hard in the Lord. Greet my dear friend Persis, another woman who has worked very hard in the Lord. 13 Greet Rufus, chosen in the Lord, and his mother, who has been a mother to me, too. 14 Greet Asyncritus, Phlegon, Hermes, Patrobas, Hermas and the brothers with them. 15 Greet Philologus, Julia, Nereus and his sister, and Olympas and all the saints with them. 16 Greet one another with a holy kiss. All the churches of Christ send greetings.

At the end of the trail, before we part ways, we have a time of greeting, words passed on to mutual friends and final words of advice and counsel. Imagine standing in a clearing at the end of a trail with the group you have been with for these past 40 days. Along the way you have discovered mutual friends that connect you. In these final moments, you pass along greetings, an action which always makes the world feel smaller than it is and binds us together in a community of familiarity. Along the way we have also talked about our struggles, our fears, and our dreams. Parting words will allude to these as we communicate our love and concern for one another as fellow travellers.

This is exactly what is happening in Acts 16. No new teachings are introduced but this is a valuable passage nonetheless, if for no other reason than it reveals a little more of the heart of the apostle. Paul mentioned 33 different people in this passage, most by name, and it is by far the longest list of greetings he includes anywhere in his epistles. Perhaps this is because he has not been to Rome but wanted to communicate a connection with these people through those they mutually knew. Reading through the list does create a feeling of community in spite of the fact that Paul had not met the Roman believers face to face.

> *Underline the names of **Phoebe** (1) and **Priscilla and Aquila** (3).*

Phoebe

Paul was writing this letter from the city of Corinth. Phoebe was a servant in the church at Cenchrae that is the port of Corinth located nine miles east of the city. She was known for her service to the Lord and was considered a deacon in her church. Paul must have known her well because he became acquainted with her plans to visit Rome. Because of her servant's heart, he knew that he could count on her to deliver the letter to the Roman church. Paul introduced her first and asked the church to receive her well for her good work for the Lord.

Perhaps you are a Phoebe. You don't preach fiery sermons or write books or articles that persuade the hearts of men and women to turn to Jesus, but you are faithful in sharing the sermons, books, articles, messages, and devotions of those who do to the ones who desperately need it. Of course the Apostle Paul was important, but without a faithful servant to carry the message along, the book of

Romans would have had little power or influence. As God exposes us to certain truths and teaching that stir our hearts and change us, let us be faithful in passing these truths along to others like Phoebe was.

Aquila & Priscilla

Starting in verse 3, Paul greeted 24 individuals who were currently residing in Rome. He began this list with Aquila and Priscilla. Of everyone on the list, we know the most about this couple. They were originally tentmakers from Rome who ended up moving to Corinth at the same time that Paul was ministering in that city. Paul ended up moving into their home in Corinth, probably because of his side job as a tentmaker. He led them to Christ and they started a church in their home. Two years later, Paul left Corinth to minister in Ephesus. Aquila and Priscilla traveled with him and started a church in their home in that city as well. Now we find this couple in Rome and, as before, hosting a church in their home. This is a great testimony of faithfulness.

Perhaps you are an Aquila or Priscilla. The gift of hospitality is used by God through you to make others comfortable and provide a place for people to come in order to hear the message of salvation. I have been in homes where the lack of hospitality clearly communicated that I was not welcomed, but I have also experienced "Aquila and Priscilla" homes that allowed me to relax and receive. The church needs these kinds of people.

The rest of the people mentioned by Paul in verses 4-16 are little known. Some of the names mirror names that are mentioned elsewhere in Paul's epistles or in historical records of the times, but lacking any concrete evidence, we cannot give much more about their stories. Suffice it to say that the list includes relatives, friends, fellow inmates, co-workers, Greek businessmen and even Paul's first Asian convert.

Paul was very comfortable with the diversity in the body of Christ. He taught that the body was made up of many members and each

member had it's own unique function. As we read through this list
of names, we begin to see the diversity in the body and we see how
Paul held each in high esteem, regardless of their position,
giftedness or ethnicity. He had taught the Romans that in Christ
there is neither male nor female, Jew nor Greek, bond nor free. He
certainly modeled this for us in his greetings.

Questions to Ponder:

1. Do you consider yourself a Phoebe? How has God used you
   in that way? Do you know others who are like Phoebe?
   How has God used them in your life?

2. Do you consider yourself an Aquila and Priscilla? How has
   God used you in that way? Do you know others who are
   like Aquila and Priscilla? How has God used them in
   your life?

3. Is the diversity in the body of Christ a blessing or a challenge
   for you?

Day 40

◆◆◆◆◆◆◆◆◆◆◆◆◆◆◆◆◆◆◆◆◆◆◆

The Purpose of the Book
(Romans 16:17-27)

17 I urge you, brothers, to watch out for those who cause divisions and put obstacles in your way that are contrary to the teaching you have learned. Keep away from them. 18 For such people are not serving our Lord Christ, but their own appetites. By smooth talk and flattery they deceive the minds of naive people. 19 Everyone has heard about your obedience, so I am full of joy over you; but I want you to be wise about what is good, and innocent about what is evil. 20 The God of peace will soon crush Satan under your feet. The grace of our Lord Jesus be with you. 21 Timothy, my fellow worker, sends his greetings to you, as do Lucius, Jason and Sosipater, my relatives. 22 I, Tertius, who wrote down this letter, greet you in the Lord. 23 Gaius, whose hospitality I and the whole church here enjoy, sends you his greetings. Erastus, who is the city's director of public works, and our brother Quartus send you their greetings. 25 Now to him who is able to establish you by my gospel and the proclamation of Jesus Christ, according to the revelation of the mystery hidden for long ages past, 26 but now revealed and made known through the prophetic writings by the command of the eternal God, so that all nations might believe and obey him-- 27 to the only wise God be glory forever through Jesus Christ! Amen.

As we continue to fellowship at the end of a long trail, we turn from words of greeting to a reminder and summary of why we made this hike. Walking away from an experience like this becomes much more meaningful when we do it with a clear understanding of the purpose we undertook when we started the trail.

> *Circle the words **cause divisions** (17), **put obstacles** (17), **smooth talk** (18), **flattery** (18), **deceive** (18) and **not serving our Lord Christ but their own appetites** (18). Highlight the phrases **keep away from them** (17) and **God of peace will soon crush Satan** (20).*

Judaizers

So much of what Paul has taught the Romans through this book has been about the influence of those who want to put Christians back under the law. Judaism under the Old Covenant was defined by the Ten Commandments and by the over 600 other laws of Moses. Many of these had to do with ceremonies and practices which had very specific instructions attached to them. Paul's message was that the New Covenant or the Gospel has set us free from the tyranny of all of these laws and rituals. However, there was evidently a group in the church at Rome that known as Judaizers, (living according to Jewish customs). These were false teachers who wanted to insist that believers were still bound by some or all of the Old Covenant regulations.

These Judaizers would not be considered true believers. There purpose was to cause division by focusing on one teaching, point of theology, or principle to the exclusion of others. By introducing certain behaviors, practices, or ceremonies, a hierarchy of Christianity could be established. The marks of a truly spiritual Christian were equated with these specific actions. Of course the end result of this kind of teaching is division. Some emphasize one teaching or behavior while others feel something else is far more important to God. The teachers of these doctrines are smooth talkers, using flattery to develop logical arguments that are designed to deceive believers into giving up their freedom in Christ and pursuing a righteousness that is defined by man. Since the teachers are the ones defining the way to get righteousness, this gives them some power of the other believers.

In the modern church culture, large groups of people are divided over issues like speaking in tongues, forbidden foods, taboo behaviors, or the celebration of holidays. The emphasis on these issues which are not really important to our faith places an obstacle in the path of Christian growth, freedom, and unity. This could not be of the Lord as it is motivated by the selfish desires of teachers who want a following and want to communicate that their way is the best or most spiritual.

Paul's advice to the Roman church is important to note. He does not encourage them to study up on the issue, engage in arguments to disprove the teachings of the Judaizers or spend time discrediting them in the assembly. He simply says we should keep away from them. In others words, we should ignore them. When we engage in these controversial conversations, we are playing right into the hands of the enemy who wants to distract us from our purpose. But if we don't refute their teachings, won't they gain the upper hand? This might happen if we didn't serve the God of truth who will cause the truth to prevail and who promises that Satan will be crushed, not by our efforts but by His power.

> *Underline the names **Timothy** (21), **Tertius** (22), **Gaius** (23) and **Erastus** (23).*

Diversity

Paul sent greetings from those who were gathered with him in Corinth. The make-up of the group highlights the diversity of the Christian converts. Timothy, of course was Paul's son in the faith who travelled with Paul, Pastored the church he founded in Ephesus, and to whom Paul wrote his final epistle from prison. Tertius, who evidently was taking dictation from Paul, was most likely a slave. His name means "third." Often slaves did not name their children but just called them by their birth order. Gaius was a leader in the city of Corinth. His hospitality is mentioned in I Corinthians. He probably housed this meeting to accommodate Paul's dictation of the letter. Finally we have Erastus, the public works director, a government official who had come to know

Christ. Paul mentioned others there whom he terms, "relatives."
Paul had family members who had come to know Christ and who
were even traveling with him on his missionary endeavors. I am
sure there were many more names of believers in Corinth that Paul
could have included. He chose these to communicate the diversity
of the group and relate to the church at Rome that their varied
cosmopolitan congregation was not completely unique.

> *Circle the words **establish** (25), **mystery** (25) and **revealed** (26).*
> *Circle the words **so that** (26) and highlight the words **believe** (26)*
> *and **obey** (26).*

In Closing

In his closing words, Paul summarizes the reason for writing this
epistle. His first desire is that the Roman believers would be
established. His purpose was that their faith would be settled on a
firm foundation. Sometimes when the family goes out to watch
fireworks on the 4th of July we take lawn chairs. The older (and
larger) you are, the more important it is to make sure that you put
your chair on level ground where all four legs are touching the
ground at the same time. If the chair is not "established" well, the
likelihood of tipping over is great! Paul wanted these believers to
have all four legs of their theology firmly planted. In another
epistle he had warned believers about being "blown about by every
wind of doctrine" (Ephesians 4:14). His teaching about the gospel,
righteousness by faith, grace and law would give them a firm
foundation upon which to live out their faith.

The key to understanding the gospel had been a mystery or
unrevealed truth. Righteousness by grace through faith, not just
for the Jews but for the whole world, was the message of the New
Covenant, revealed through the apostles and prophets and the
writings of the New Testament. The mystery was no longer a
mystery, it was the revelation of the gospel of Christ.

Paul's final goal in writing this epistle is introduced by the words
so that in verse 26. Paul wanted them to understand the gospel but

not just *so that* they would have a deeper knowledge. He wanted them to understand the gospel *so that* they (and the world) would believe the gospel and obey it. Paul's heartbeat was to help people understand the truth of the gospel *so that* they would embrace it and become true followers of Jesus Christ.

These last verses may be helpful as an evaluation tool for our own personal ministry. Why do we study the Bible? Why do we teach the Bible to others? Why do we attend church? Paul's answer would be that we do these things *so that* we and others can be established, know the truth about the Gospel to the end that others believe and obey it. Period. Not to make a name for ourselves. Not to build a big ministry. Not to prove a point.

This is the end of the trail. It has been great journeying with you through this book. I close with Paul's words, "...to the only wise God be glory forever through Jesus Christ! Amen!"

Questions to Ponder:

1. What is the significance of the names Paul mentioned in verses 21-24?

2. What does Paul reveal about his purpose in writing this epistle?

3. Have you believed and obeyed the gospel?

40873737R00139

Made in the USA
Lexington, KY
21 April 2015